"Urgent and brutal."
—The New York Times Book Review

W9-CDZ-308

**"A love letter
to survivors."**
—Bustle

**"Anderson uses
her experience
to light a path
for others to
find purpose."**
—TIME

**"A masterclass in
feminism, in story-
telling, and the
power of words."**
—Book Riot

**"A searing
memoir about
long-suppressed
secrets, trauma
and rage."**
—San Francisco
Chronicle

**"These stark,
beautiful poems
will break
your heart."**
—NPR Book Concierge

A NEW YORK TIMES BESTSELLER!

praise for
SHOUT

"These stark, beautiful poems will break your heart, take your breath away and beg to be underlined, highlighted and dog-eared."　　　　—NPR Book Concierige

"With *Speak* Anderson opened the door for more novels exploring the deeply felt and deeply personal aftermath of sexual violence. *SHOUT* serves as both a testament to the life-altering, lifesaving impact of these types of stories— and as an urgent and brutal reminder of their ongoing necessity."　　　　*—The New York Times Book Review*

"[Anderson's] poems raise urgent alarms, warning against the evils propagated by a culture that values dominance over respect . . . Anderson uses her experiences to light a path for others to find purpose."　　　　*—TIME*

"*SHOUT* weaves stories about formative experiences with meditations on sexual violence, boundaries, and gender dynamics to paint a clear and poignant picture of the insidiousness of rape culture and the lessons it teaches us."
—Bitch

"Anderson's prose is so gorgeous . . . that at times the book needs to be put down to absorb her utter mastery of language."　　　　*—Entertainment Weekly*

"Haunting, vulnerable, and striking . . . Both a love letter to survivors and a call-to-action, *SHOUT* is a necessary read of the #MeToo era." —Bustle

"Absolutely essential . . . A book of staggering importance." —Refinery29

"Brilliant, beautiful." —*Marie Claire*

"Inspiring." —*Cosmopolitan*

"Flawless . . . A masterclass in feminism, in storytelling, and in the power of words to draw action that changes the world." —Book Riot

"[A] searing memoir about long-suppressed secrets, trauma and rage . . . Breathtaking turns of phrase amplify candor around violations and violence, silence and shame, guilt and rage." —*San Francisco Chronicle*

"Anderson brings to the fore again and again the devastation that silence about sexual abuse can cause . . . We might understand *SHOUT* as an exorcism that recognizes the damage done as a way to cleanse it." —*Los Angeles Review of Books*

"Anderson is a brilliant writer, and her fiery memoir is a voice we need to hear." —*The Buffalo News*

"There is grief, rage, and power in every word . . . An incredible book." —Bookish

★ "A captivating, powerful read about clawing your way out of trauma . . . Fervent and deafening."

—*Booklist*, starred review

★ "Powerful . . . alternately raw and lyrical."

—*Publishers Weekly*, starred review

★ "An important book for the #MeToo movement. Necessary for every home, school, and public library."

—*Kirkus Reviews*, starred review

★ "Ferociously raw . . . [a] deeply personal look into how [Anderson] channeled her pain into the writing of *Speak*."

—*BookPage*, starred review

★ "Immensely powerful, *SHOUT* is for everyone."

—Shelf Awareness, starred review

★ "Will ring out to readers who themselves believe in the power of stories."

—*The Bulletin of the Center for Children's Books*, starred review

★ "Searing . . . More than a gifted writer, Anderson is an advocate for anyone who feels alienated. Her sensitive, incisive book is essential for all young people."

—*School Library Journal*, starred review

★ "A praise song to survivors, a blistering rebuke to predators, and a testament to the healing power of shared stories."

—*The Horn Book*, starred review

★ "A collective masterpiece."

—*School Library Connection*, starred review

awards and accolades

A *New York Times* Bestseller

Longlisted for the 2019 National Book Award

A 2019 Goodreads Choice Award Winner

A *TIME* Best Book of the Year

An NPR Best Book of the Year

An Amazon Best Book of the Year

A New York Public Library Best Book of the Year

A Chicago Public Library Best Book of the Year

A #1 Spring Indie Next List Pick

A *Publishers Weekly* Best Book of the Year

A *Kirkus Reviews* Best Book of the Year

A Shelf Awareness Best Book of the Year

A *Horn Book* Best Book of the Year

A *Booklist* Best Book of the Year

An *SLJ* Best Book of the Year

A *BCCB* Best Book of the Year

also by
laurie halse anderson

SHOUT

a poetry memoir

LAURIE
HALSE
ANDERSON

PENGUIN BOOKS

PENGUIN BOOKS
An imprint of Penguin Random House LLC, New York

First published in the United States of America by Viking,
an imprint of Penguin Random House LLC, 2019
Published by Penguin Books, an imprint of Penguin Random House LLC, 2020

Visit us online at penguinrandomhouse.com

LIBRARY OF CONGRESS CATALOGING-IN-PUBLICATION DATA IS AVAILABLE

ISBN 9780142422205

Printed in the United States of America

10 9 8 7 6 5 4 3 2

for the survivors

SHOUT

introduction

Finding my courage to speak up twenty-five years after I was raped, writing *Speak*, and talking with countless survivors of sexual violence made me who I am today.

This book shows how that happened.

It's filled with the accidents, serendipities, bloodlines, tidal waves, sunrises, disasters, passport stamps, criminals, cafeterias, nightmares, fever dreams, readers, portents, and whispers that have shaped me so far.

My father wrote poetry, too. He gave me these guidelines: we must be gentle with the living, but the dead own their truth and are fearless. So I've written honestly about the challenges my parents faced and how their struggles affected me. The poems that reference people other than me or my family are truth told slant; I've muddled specific details to protect the identities of survivors.

This is the story of a girl who lost her voice and wrote herself a new one.

PRELUDE: mic test

this book smells like me
woodsmoke
salt
honey and strawberries
sunscreen, libraries
failures and sweat
green nights in the mountains
cold dawns by the sea

this book reeks
of my fear
of depression's black dogs howling
and the ancient shames riding
my back, their claws
buried deep

this book is yesterday's mud
dried on the dance floor
the step patterns
cautiously submitted
for your curious investigation
of what I feel like
on the inside

one

in the name of love

When he was eighteen years old, my father
saw his buddy's head sliced into two pieces,
sawn just above the eyebrows by an exploding
brake drum, when he was in the middle
of telling a joke.

Repairing planes, P-51s, on an air base in England,
hungry for a gun, not a wrench, my father
pushed an army-issue trunk into his mind
and put the picture of his friend's last breath
at the bottom of it.

Then they sent him to Dachau.
Not just him, of course, his whole unit,
and not just to Dachau, but to all of the camps
because the War was over.
But not really.

Daddy didn't talk to me for forty years
about what he saw, heard, what he smelled
what he did about it;

one year of silence for every day of the Flood,
one year for every day from Lent until Easter.

The air in Dachau was clouded with the ash
from countless bodies, as he breathed it in
the agony of the dying infected my father,
and all of his friends. They tried to help
the suffering, followed orders, took out their
rage in criminal ways while their officers
turned away. My father filled the trunk
in his head with walking corpses who sang
to him every night for the rest of his life.

One day Daddy watched a pregnant woman
walking slowly down the road
near the gates of Dachau
he matched his steps to hers,
then stopped as she crouched in a ditch
and birthed a baby.

My father, a kid on the verge of destruction,
half-mad from the violence he'd seen
desperate to kill, to slaughter, to maim,
watched that baby slip into the world

between her momma's blood-slicked thighs
and it healed him just enough
that he wept.

He wrapped the newborn in her mother's apron
and helped them both to the Red Cross tent
set up for survivors.

stained glass curtains in my mother's mouth

Veteran of D/depression,
the German war and atrocities
a handsome boy married the tall girl
who looked like Katharine Hepburn
two kids adrift in a city far from home
two ships ripped from their moorings.

Mom told me the story when I was in high school,
on a night when Daddy's drinking
drove our family to the edge
"He had to slap me," she said. "It happened
before you were born."

The image of my father hitting
my mother picassoed in front of me
like Sunday sunshine slicing
through the church windows, fracturing
and rearranging the truth on the floor.

They lived in Boston back then
Daddy studying to be a preacher

Mom trying to be a wife.
"He had to slap me," she repeated.
"I was screaming,"
screaming for reasons
too many to count.

The full story came out in gingerbread
crumbs dropped to show me the way.

After the meltdown, the attack,
they had to ride the train home
to repair the damage to her face
home to the mountains, to their parents
to a clucking village of spite,
her broken teeth vibrating
in bloody sockets,
her husband horrified at the war
he'd declared on his beloved,
he turned toward the aisle
thinking of escape.

Her backbone crumbling
under the weight of her heart,
she fixed her eyes on the dark
forest just beyond the glass.

"I wouldn't shut up,"
she said. "He had to."

The lie told to friends was that she fell,
clumsy, tumbled down the stairs
so many broken teeth, poor thing
bad things happen
in big cities, you know.

The truth was that the stress
of fighting the ghosts in his head
broke him that night
and as they argued
my father didn't just slap my mother.
He beat her.
But beatings didn't fit in the fairy tales
she liked to tell herself
so she sugarcoated the story
to make it easier to swallow.

The town dentist, a family friend,
didn't charge for his labor
gently apologized with every tooth.
They lived with her parents all summer

while her mouth healed,
waiting for the false teeth, they tiptoed
but they did not touch.

After the stitches came out
after she learned to mix
tooth powder with water
to make the glue
that held her mouth together,
after five miscarriages,
five never-born sons,
my parents tried again
and created me. He didn't ever hit
her again, but she lived in the fear
that he would, which had everything to do
with her habits of silence.

unclean

I said "shit"
in front of the church ladies
gathered in our kitchen
for coffee and doughnuts,
three-year-old me:
the potato-shaped, sturdy-legged
parrot-tongued echo chamber

I fell down, scraped my knee,
and said "shit" in frustration,
the word I had learned
from my mother
crammed and dammed
into the corseted life
of a minister's wife
where she couldn't say
"shit"
if she had a mouthful.

But alone,
with me,

she could, and did
frequently.

That day in the kitchen,
as the church ladies
eyed my mother's handmade
curtains, measuring her skills,
I baby-cursed and was snatched from the floor.

Shoving a bar of soap into the mouth of a child
was then a common practice, church lady approved,
for scrubbing dirty words from the minds
of the young, the violence
of generational silence
brutally handed down.

Ivory grooves deep-carved
in the bar by my baby teeth
Mommy's bruising fingers
pinning me against the sink

My sobs captured in bubbles
heard only after they popped,
after I was jailed in my room

and the ladies of the church and my mother
sipped bitterness and shared crumbs.

I learned then that words
had such power
some must never be spoken
and was thus robbed of both
tongue and the truth.

earthbound

My mother took me to a pond
when I was four years old
for swimming lessons. There was a beach,
of sorts, littered with pine needles and mothers
smoking cigarettes on towels,
wearing sweaters and warm socks;
summer in the North Country.

Mom tugged off my sweatshirt and shooed me
toward the crowd of kids standing
at water's edge. The Lady of the Lake,
our swimming teacher, a giantess topped
with a rubber bathing cap studded
with plastic flowers,
began the lesson.

On our bellies, facing the beach,
hands in the mud
legs in the water, my feet motorboated obediently.
I didn't mind kicking long as I could hold
on to the shore.

But then the Lady beckoned us into deep water
one by one. I refused,
even with the rest of the class staring.
The Lady hooked me under the armpits and pulled
me in.

Never trust anyone with plastic flowers
on their head.

I hollered so loud the Lady consulted
with my mother,
the other moms clucking and whispering.
I won
the position at the shallowest edge of the pond
where I pulled through a few inches of water
with my hands in the earth,
occasionally waving an arm in the air to pretend
like I was swimming,
a stubborn tadpole
suspicious of the deep.

directionally challenged

In first grade we moved
country mouse to the city
whiskers quivering, eyes wide,
couple days later Mom put my sister
in the stroller and we three
walked through a drizzle of gold
and ruby leaves up one hill, down
another to the new school, made of bricks,
registered in the office, Mom handed me
my lunch box and waved
a fast goodbye

I sat in the back row, played
hopscotch with some girls, and ran
hands in the air as the bell rang at day's end
followed the crowd out the door,
the crossing guard our white-gloved guardian,
I walked down the block
in the wrong direction

Stopped.
Back to the intersection, ninety-degree turn

went up the hill, that felt better
until it didn't
until the houses were the wrong shape to hold
my family.
Stopped.

Back to the intersection, worried, then down the
third street, the wrong third way.
Stopped. Back to the intersection
the fourth spoke of the wheel another mistake.
Last kid in sight, country mouse,
five years old, spinning
at the center of a compass that had lost
her true north

A white glove waved, the guard crouched
wings tucked neatly behind her back,
eyes all-seeing
she wiped my tears and took my hand
and led me
up the hill again, gold and ruby leaves,
farther than I'd dared on my own tiny paws,

until we crested and scurried
down the other side and the houses
changed shape and at the very bottom
of the hill stood my new home
my mother waiting at the curb.

practice

Mr. Irving styled and helmeted my mom's hair
introduced her to the other ladies, permed,
perfumed, fuming about their husbands
the confessor hairdresser, he knew all
the juicy details. Told Mom I should join
the city swim team, cuz all the kids did
and it would make me tired enough
to sleep better at night, and not spend
so much time in her hair.

There was a slight delay in joining the team
while I learned to swim in water deeper
than six inches. But then I traded muddy ponds
for cement swimming pools in schools
and parks all over the city, tadpoling
backstroking, butterflying, freestyling
until my body leaned, gleamed, hardened
into a core of speed
with a snaggletoothed grin.
Didn't care much about winning,
but I hated to come in last, my sweet spot

was lane seven for long, slow miles of laps
punctuated by flip turns
boom!
powering underwater, mermaid made real
I felt my gills growing
I could breathe without air.

chum

Underwater, city
swimming pool

a shiver of slippery boys
eleven, twelve years old
with shark-toothed fingers
and gap-toothed smiles
isolate
the openhearted girls
eight, nine years old
tossed in like bloody
buckets of chum.

The boys circle, then frenzy-feed
crotch-grabbing, chest-pinching,
hate-spitting
the water afroth
with glee and destruction.

Girls stay in the shallows
after their baptism as bait,

that first painful lesson
in how lifeguards
look the other way.

lovebrarians

I hated reading. Loathed the ants
swarming across the page, lost
my excitement about school, fought, reduced
to a puzzle with missing pieces.
Once branded, the feeling of stupid never fades
no matter how many medals you win.

But then we rode the bus downtown
me and Leslie, who majored in music
and lived in our attic, Mary Poppins
with a Jersey accent, we rode the bus downtown,
the coins hot from my hand *plink, plink*
in the box next to the driver, all the way downtown
to a Carnegie library built by an immigrant
so everyone could read, free
and untrammeled by politicians seeking
to bind them into ignorance,
chain them to the wheel.
Leslie promised she'd read me the books
so I didn't have to be afraid of mistakes
and I wrote My Name in big letters

got my first badge, a library card
I asked the librarian
"Can I take out all the books?"
and she answered quite seriously
"Of course, dear,
just not at the same time."

And so, with extra Leslie help and a chorus
of angels disguised as teachers and librarians
for years unstinting with love and hours
of practice, those ants finally marched
in straight lines for me
shaped words, danced sentences,
constructed worlds
for a girl finally learning how to read

I unlocked the treasure chest
and swallowed the key.

poem for my favorite teacher

Mrs. Sheedy-Shea
taught me haiku, I word-flew
off the page, amazed

hippos

indoctrinated by magazine covers of skeletal
white privilege like the Kennedys
(only peasants ate, apparently)
my parents, poor-clanned and striving
rose to the occasion and smothered
my hunger
by pinching my hips
grabbing the fat under my chin
when I was eight years
ten, fourteen
twenty-five hungry years old
when they grabbed and pinched
they called me "Baby Hippo"
the insult disguised as
love, they said others would tease
me for being so fat
so I might as well
get used to it

closeted shame

When we were girls we rode horses
disguised as bicycles
though anyone with eyes could see from the way
we leaned, preened their manes, galloped
across the plains without ever leaving
Dorset Avenue, their true equine nature
we were magic-filled girls at large
in a world of pedestrian dullness.

After riding hard, we'd walk to cool
down our steeds, feed them sugar cubes, pump
their tires, straighten the playing cards
in the spokes
that made the *thwacka-thwacka-thwacka-thwack*
announcing our arrival, knees always skinned,
crusted with scabs from tripping
over the buckled sidewalk that was heaved
into the air by killing frosts and held there
by the roots of long-dead trees,
left broken to teach children
lessons about watching our step.

I used my jump rope for reins and a lasso
for runaway calves, and the whirling dervish
of girl games, sky-jumping, earth-touching,
clap-backing
shouted with rhymes. We got tangled
up a lot and fell,
splitting open our half-healed knees, we licked
our bloody wounds clean
and started all over again.

My bike had a shelf on the back, an ornament,
I guess, but made of metal. One day,
I let a friend's little sister ride on the back
of my horse
on that shelf, her shoelaces tangled
in the spokes, her leg twisted
at a horrible angle, then broke.
Her screams drove
me to the linen closet, where I hid for hours,
sobbing
burning with the horror
that I'd hurt her, not my fault, but yes,
totally my fault, and she wore a heavy cast for
months.

I stopped playing horses after that.

The taste of shame smells
like stubborn vomit in your hair
lingering no matter how often you wash it
sometimes you have to shave
yourself bald
and start again like a newly hatched chick
leaving the faint rot of broken magic
in shattered eggshell pieces
behind you.

payback

After *Charlotte's Web*
but before *Little Women*,
my sister stole the key
to my green plastic diary,
and blackmailed me
with what she found

We shared a room split in two
with masking tape laid down
the middle of the floor,
and the closet, the lines
never to be crossed

I hadn't committed felonies
or misdemeanors, yet; I was in fifth grade
but still, she tattled about what I wrote
how I'd cheated in math
and planned to do it again

I repaid her treachery
by telling stories in the dark
while we waited for sleep,

said I was a vampire, the moles
on my neck proved it,
part werewolf, too, casting
stories by the light of the moon
until she cried for Mom
who yelled at me for scaring
my sister, and grounded
me so I never did it again
but I threatened to
whenever she crashed
through the border

Maybe I owe her,
my sister,
for stealing the key, toying
with my secrets, and thus igniting
the slow-fused inevitability
of me weaving stories
in the dark

amplified

1. Daddy loved Jesus, talked about Him so much when I was little I thought He was a cousin, maybe just a second cousin, which would explain why He was never at Grandma's for Thanksgiving. Daddy was a preacher on a college campus, he worked in the chapel and I could walk there by myself to say hello if I looked both ways before I crossed the street.

2. My job was school, I was really good at recess and lunch, but I failed climbing the rope that hung from the sky in gym. I tried to be sick every Friday so I wouldn't fail the spelling bee. The playground was a war of girls versus boys and now I feel shame cuz some kids must have wanted to stand with the other team, and some must have wanted new teams entirely, but the world was drawn for us binary in clumsy chalk lines, and we'd try to do better when we were in charge.

3. Protests against the Vietnam War echoed across the campus, our house filled with angry students

every weekend, and my mom fed them vats of spaghetti and trays of brownies. Daddy worked all the time because students were getting so high they thought they could fly and they jumped out of dorm windows five stories up, which was awful, and the sadness and the rage and the protests and the soldiers and the yelling and the guns and the FBI tapping our phone and the corpses of Dachau made it hard for Daddy to sleep and he could smell the ashes again and my mom thought he was killing himself and he was, but he was doing it in slow motion.

4. I finally learned to read and they finally integrated our school and the new kids were really nice and long division was impossible and my mother cut my hair wicked short cuz swimming and everyone thought I was a boy which was NOT FUNNY because I wasn't and I didn't want to be one. Boys were gross.

5. Daddy was a delegate to the Democratic National Convention and he forced us to listen to the Watergate hearings on the radio, he hated Richard Nixon with all of his heart and soul; when drunk, Daddy threatened to kill the son of a bitch because he was destroying the country. I watched the level of gin

in the bottle and realized that counting the bottles was more important.

6. Spring of sixth grade, all of us crammed into the music room, sticky hot and stinky cuz we were almost seventh graders and the chairs were too small and our hormones were blowing UP. But we were children. Who smelled. It was a confusing time. Our music teacher, Mrs. Schermerhorn, dragged us through a rehearsal for the Spring Musical Performance That No One Wanted to Hear. We were terrible singers and horrible children, but

something happened

the planets lining up, gods playing cosmic checkers, a butterfly flapping in Bangladesh

she made us sing "Climb Ev'ry Mountain," yeah, that one, from *Sound of Music*, when Maria and her family stop in a convent as they are escaping the Nazis, a song about doing hard things, we sang that song without fooling and when we were finished Mrs. Schermerhorn coughed, cleared her throat, warned us not to move, and she ran out

(of course we moved and gossiped and complained and farted and rolled our eyes it was June and we only had a few days left).

7. This all went down right around the time my parents stopped worrying about things like school concerts and report cards. I thought I was the only kid with a house on fire, but I wasn't.

8. Mrs. Schermerhorn returned with our principal, Miss Hartnett, and she told us to sing again. Nervous, too many yearlings in a small corral, we didn't want to obey, but we had no choice, we sang
    letting go
    opening
and ninetyish voices, some cracking, some strained under weights unseen, murmurated, a flock of swooping starlings, harmonizing, resonating, shaking the windows in the pain, bending the laws of physics to the pure hearts of children for the length of a song from a Broadway musical
    that made two brilliant, kind, ignored women cry
    briefly
    and lifted us to a place we weren't old enough to understand.

first blood

When husbands raped wives
in 1972, it was legal.
Property rights were all the rage
you know.

> I got my first period
> in 1972 and
> I didn't know why
> I was bleeding.

When bosses groped women
in 1972, it was legal
because bosses
(all of them male)
made the rules.

> We girls saw a filmstrip
> in 1972, about
> hygiene and sanitary napkins,
> so confusing because
> it never mentioned
> the blood.

When women were fired
in 1972
because they got pregnant

in 1972,
it was all very legal
in 1972,
no questions were ever asked.

                    We learned boys
                    were dangerous,
                in 1972, cuz their pee
                could get us pregnant
                and kicked out of school.
The FBI spied on women
in 1972, and it was legal.
Men feared the liberation
movement might change
all of the rules.

                    My mother lacked a mouth
                    in 1972, so she couldn't
                    explain the mystery
                    of the blood.
                    She gave me a
                    pink box of tampons,
                directions hidden inside,
                    then closed the door
                    between us.
                    No words.

fencing

Levy Junior High, seventh grade
long, dark walks to school on winter mornings
world deep-bundled in snow, the game
was to scuttle into the street, grab hold
of the back bumper of a school bus
or the bread truck,
let it pull us down the frozen roads
of Syracuse, sliding toward the Eleusinian
mysteries of adolescence. Mom hated
that school cuz of the knife fight, but I liked
it, though my shyness limited me to the sidelines,
you can learn a lot from watching quietly
a great art teacher taught us
how much fun it is to make things
from scratch

Eighth grade, another year, another school
me, the quiet scholarship kid,
Mom was happy cuz there were no knife fights
there, no fights of any kind, unless you count the
upper-school cutthroat competition
for valedictorian

I was a cheerleader, can you believe it?
One-third of the base of a girl pyramid
pom-pommed in modest, itchy uniforms
I learned to fence with an épée
studied sumacs, danced the steps of fragile
friendships, but it was Mr. Edwards
who changed my life,
he didn't just teach us Greek mythology,
Mr. Edwards ensorcelled us
with stories of gods and wars, mothers
in search of lost daughters,
and girls fleeing rapists
by turning into trees
I wanted to stay in that school
forever

cemetery girl

When not swimming, my middle
school summers played
out in Oakwood Cemetery
where I lay
on a flat, warm tomb
day after day
and
read read read read read read
book-belly starving
for pages fantastical,
haunted by lost
hungry girls,
I ate red apples
heavy-salted on the tomb
the sleeping Victorian corpses
below fed me secrets
sentinel owls peered
from a grove of old pines,
all of us hoping, waiting on signs
of the change
that was promised

driven

My father first let me drive when I was twelve
in the woods on old logging trails,
only a couple times in town
when he was over the limit.

I drove in sheer terror
never crashed
not even a scratch in the paint
he was proud of me
and that meant a lot.

My mother never knew
that we forged a secret alliance
in the middle of our
Cold War nuclear-family meltdown
so when it was time for her
to teach me how to drive
I faked it, pretending
I didn't have a clue.

ante-crescendo

My mother hit me in the face
for the last time
when my father lost his job
lost us to the wildfire
that scorched the dining room table
burned up the drapes
while bombs dropped through the ceiling

You have to seriously screw up
to be fired by the Church
cuz love, Jesus, etc.
plus plenty of preachers play
out shame mistakes in glass houses
so they rarely throw stones
but my dad, he was targeted
by petty jealousies and for dumb mistakes,
they called him on the carpet
and wiped the floor with him
subtle, ceremonious excommunication
bell, book, and candlewise
Dad's pedestal tipped

over and he had a great fall
and all of the king's horses
and all of the king's men
didn't give a damn

I argued with him about something stupid
so confused that our life was in flames
Dad told me to shut up, as he stormed off
I stuck out my tongue at his retreating form
just as Mom came around the corner,
with a mean backhand and explosive temper
she hit me

I was almost as tall as she was,
just as angry
and much, much stronger

we stared at each other
after the blow, on the edge
of annihilation, wordless
combustion
but she was my mother
so I swallowed the lighter fluid

and tilted my head
until my face became her mirror

like I said,
that was the last time
she hit me

packing for exile

We lived in the house on Berkeley Drive
for seven years, long enough to sucker
me into believing that was a home
my mistake
when you're a preacher's kid, you move
around a lot, don't get to paint your walls
or tape up posters; the Church buys the furniture
pays the mortgage and makes all the rules.

Dad sort of disappeared.
No,
actually, he vanished
leaving my mother
to move us
like Hercules, charged with cleaning
the shit-filled stables of King Augeas, she wrestled
a fast-flowing river for the dirty work
refusing to carry the past with us
she threw it all away
stacks of hymnals
her trombone

generations of family letters
quilts, handmade syrup buckets
photographs that made her eyes bleed
chicken pot pies from the freezer
she threw out the memories of Christmases
without tears
the night she went on a rare date with my father
when she wore a black dress with a white collar
perfumed with Joy, lemon-tanged
she tossed out watching the astronauts walk
on the moon
my sister's broken arm
me singing into a hairbrush
she dumped out Grandpa's search for his shotgun
when he realized the electroshock
treatment wasn't working, she trashed
camping in the woods, fireflies dancing
marshmallows toasting over the fire
the only thing we packed in the moving truck
were our carapaces pinned
like specimens to a corkboard

IT, part 1—gasoline

Remember the line in *Speak*,
"And I thought for just a minute there that . . .
I would start high school with a boyfriend"?
Yeah, that was me
for a couple naive days
when I was
thirteen years old.

We moved in June
four shards of a family,
one apartment of burnt
orange and avocado green,
two bedrooms.

I bought the *Goodbye Yellow Brick Road*
album with my babysitting money. The boy
across the street had a motorbike
he syphoned gas for it every night
the trick, he said,
was only to take a little
from each car,
that way no one noticed.

He grabbed me
once.
Pushed me against a
brick wall, hands greased
with experience
arms metal cables
looping around and encasing me.

I fought, tried to kick
and failed, his mouth dove
for my neck and
I bit him
until I tasted blood.

He backed off, furious
cried that human bites
were germ-filled, poisonous.
I said I hoped that was true.

That boy tasted gasoline dangerous,
but he wasn't IT.
My sour victory
did not last long.

IT, part 2—trees

We moved to a new
building a few weeks later, I
made friends with girls who shared
candy-flavored lip gloss and giggly fantasies
about Vinnie Barbarino and the Fonz
girls who introduced me to IT,
the friend of a friend of a friend
cuz everyone is your friend when
you're thirteen and alone.

Broken children
can see each other from miles away,
the original mutants, X-kids abandoned
to their confused scars and rages. I held
his hand, enjoyed our silent summer
swooping circles of bewilderment. Not romance
but comfort, to have a tobacco-smelling
boy, older, bigger, stronger boy
walk by my side.

Looking back, I think his life was a mess.
Looking back, he still scares me.

Looking back, I wonder how many girls
he hurt
and if someone hurt him first
or if he was simply a felony-committing
shithead.

And then green August, melting-hot
days running out the bottom of the hour-
glass, school time marching
relentlessly toward the children of
summer so intent on capturing
every free minute, like flowers
to be pressed between the pages
of a book. We walked down
the hill to the creek, far away from the heat,
the trees our shade companions, the babble
of water overrunning any need to speak
we tossed pebbles in the water
everything was so calm that's what I
remember the calm cuz I was safe
and happy tossing pebbles in the water
next to this tobacco-smelling boy
friend,
so when he turned to kiss
me

my mouth met his with delight, I was new
to this kind of kiss and happy to play
by the creek with this boy whose hands then
wandered fast, too fast, too far
like a flash flood overwhelming the startled
banks of a creek that never once thought
of defense, of damming or the need for a bridge
to escape
his hands, arms shoulders back
muscle sinew bone
an avalanche of force
the course predetermined one hand on my mouth
his body covering smothering mine
I took my eyes off the rage
in his face and looked up to the green peace
of leaves fluttering above, trees witnessing
pain shame I crawled into the farthest corner
of my mind biding time hiding surviving
by outsiding

and when he was done
using my body
he stood and zipped his jeans
lit a cigarette
and walked away.

IT, part 3—playing chicken with the devil

Lots of boys at our school played chicken
the shifting pecking order of coward and stud
beating a dark bass note in the cold current
of doubt that flowed through their hearts.

One boy lost a game of Russian roulette
for real,
a revolver, six chambers, one bullet
loaded, then spun so no one knew
where it was hiding, the gun
went hand to hand to hand, following the snake-
smoke path of the bong,
laughing, basement smelling of mold
and boy farts, cheap beer, and the gun goes *click*,
to the next hand *click*, to the next hand
before the laughter fades,

BAM.

It didn't kill him. He was smart
enough to tilt the barrel at an obtuse

angle, so the bullet only stole his memories
chewed through his charm and blinded him.
He was a quiet, kind fixture
in the empty garage
where we smoked between classes,
sheltered from the cold,
his black hair long to cover the scars,
white cane in his hand,
old friends standing guard.

Lots of boys at my school played chicken,
countless varieties of the game.

The boy who raped me
on the rocks by the creek
got drunk and lay down
twenty-eight nights later
on a dark country road
he played chicken with the devil,
daring the car that couldn't see him
to flinch first, to prove him brave
and noble.

I didn't speak up
when that boy raped me, instead I scalded

myself in the shower and turned
me into the ghost of the girl
I once was, my biggest fear
being that my father,
no stranger to gaming
with the devil,
would kill that boy

and it would be my fault.

But that boy who raped me
on the rocks by the creek
got drunk and lay down
on a dark night to play
chicken with the devil
and he lost.

I begged my father
to take me to the funeral. I lied
and said that boy was my friend.

He looked at me sharply,
my ice-eyed father
my gentle-hearted father, he heard
something in my voice

but after one searing glance, he shut
down the inquiry
wrote the note
got me out
of school and walked with me
to the graveside on
a gray September day cut by winter's
promise in the wind.

My father kept his arm
around my shoulders, while I cried
so hard I turned myself inside
out, so grateful IT was gone
and it was over.

I did not know
that the haunting
had just begun.

clocks melting on the floor

I didn't think about pregnancy
for weeks, when it finally hit me
I puked and cried, afraid
that I was puking
cuz there was a baby
but the next day I bled
a stormy river, so grateful
didn't think about STIs
didn't know what they were
to be honest
after I was raped
I could hardly think at all
because feelings hid in the closet,
under the bed, shadow-cloaked
and hungry, dark mountains
and oceans of noise threatened
to spill over if I opened
my mouth, I was afraid
I'd never stop screaming

pain management

My parents drank fury and gin
when we lived in places
quick-rented, half-furnished
with couches and beds that smelled
of strangers, the floors scrubbed
with regret.

A wolf, when wounded, retreats
to a dark place, burns out the injury
with fever, lies still so the bones
can knit back together,
or dies alone.
But we were not wolves.

We moved
and moved again, being not-wolves,
with our legs snapped in the metal
trap jaws, livers pecked each night
by eagles,
my parents broke

themselves on the wheels of time and
appearances, drunk
on gin and fury, they ossified.

Of course I got high.

buzzed

giggled
ate molasses cookies baked—*ha, I said "baked"*—
by my grandmother
drank music: Boston Bob Seger Black Sabbath
Blue Öyster Cult Supertramp Doobie Brothers
Allman Brothers Bill Withers Eagles
Stevie Wonder Steely Dan Lynyrd Skynyrd
Aerosmith
Temptations Santana Genesis Led Zeppelin
Fleetwood Mac
landsliding through my bones
sloooooooooooooooooooooooooooooooooow
I drew pictures
x-ed them, rejected them with a black magic
marker, threw them in the garbage

weed buzz dulled *thankyouthankyouthankyouthankyouthankyou*
the pain, verdigris skeleton key
turned in my brain's rusty lock
I understood
I could fucking *see* the connections
'tween everything and everybody, the

four—
no, the five-dimensional chessboard
we danced on
I scribbled notes in crayon
messages in bottles cast
into the sea of me
then lost in the deep
I got high to escape
sat in sunshine, eyes closed
wanted to peel back my lids,
but I knew a girl who did that,
dead-crazy high on smack
(not weed)
she had pale eyes to begin with, almost as white
as her hair, so when she, dead-crazy high, opened
her eyes for a staring contest with the sun
the sun won
and she couldn't see too good after that
but she got sober,
for sure
I kept my eyes closed
after smoking, usually fell asleep,
bored and stuck
in hardening concrete
up to my chin

ninth grade: my year of living stupidly

1. I forgot to go to class a lot, even for subjects like French and social studies that I enjoyed. When I remembered to go, it was hard to stay awake cuz I wasn't sleeping good at night. At first I'd hide in the fantasy section of the library when I forgot to go to class. Then I met some kids who lived a few blocks from school and they were happy to share high afternoons listening to music with me, all of us pretending we weren't doomed.

2. Concrete burns are lethal. Sneaky, too. Stick your hands or feet into wet concrete and it feels like a milkshake. You'd never guess you were going to need an amputation.

3. I didn't have real friends because a friend is someone you trust and trust never came easy after that boy raped me. But I had people to get high with, people to share sandwiches with. Some-

times I had people to walk with in the halls. Being mocked doesn't hurt as much when someone
walks next to you. I was grateful for my almost-
friends.

4. It's all about the pH levels. Vinegar is an acid,
pH 2.4; skin is acid, too, pH 5.5. Wet concrete is
wicked alkaline, pH 12.0; that's caustic enough to
eat you alive.

5. They called us dirtbags: the clan of X-kids who
smelled of cigarettes and weed and farm work and
clothes worn without washing because the laun-
dromat was expensive and the priority was staying
warm. We weren't the only ones whose parents were
drunk or violent or absent . . . but we were the poor
kids dealing with that shit. Our school was organized by income brackets, with the kids who skied
in Colorado over winter break at the top and the
dirtbags at the bottom.

6. It was probably more complicated than that, but
that's what it felt like sitting in the shadows at the
base of the social mountain.

7. The concrete keeps burning even after you wash it off your skin. The gift that keeps on giving, the death that keeps on deathing.

8. Once I sat in the backseat of a Chevy with four other people; there were three more up front, plus the driver, and we were profoundly wasted and we drove around the rim of an old quarry and something happened cuz suddenly the driver took us straight back to his house and didn't say anything for the rest of the night. Next day I went back there and found our tracks; we'd come inches from plunging to the bottom. I didn't hang out with those guys after that.

9. Concrete burns through your skin and your meat, then it burns down to your bones if you don't get help.

10. One night I mixed cheap whiskey with spiced Russian tea that tasted like moldy oranges. Numbing drunk was what we did in my family when horrible things happened that we didn't talk about, like being fired, or having the electricity shut off,

or Mom eating cereal for dinner so we could have the hamburger. Or being raped; we definitely didn't talk about rape. Ever. The color I vomited for hours after those drinks was really quite astounding. I still can't touch whiskey or spiced Russian tea.

11. I started being stupid to turn down the volume of my internal emergency alert system. But blundering stupid through life makes everything way more complicated, creates cascading avalanches of new problems.

12. I wasn't just encased in hardening concrete up to my chin; it was pouring down my throat. I was in a race to see if I would die from the outside in or the inside out.

diagnosis

I knew that if I fell and scraped my knee
ejected headfirst through a windshield
chopped off a finger or lost a leg to a shark
I'd apply pressure to stop the bleeding
use towels, blankets, Goodwill sweaters
whatever it took to start clotting,
slow the fluid loss
I'd close my wounds with fishhooks and twine
or a stapler or a nail gun
welding torch to reconnect my spine
I'd knit skin grafts, if necessary.
After I pulled myself back together
I'd need a doctor cuz my dark corners
would be invaded
by bacteria, viruses, parasites, and more,
infectious
vectors of disease, some lethal, some merely
debilitating, chronic cripplers.
I knew that. I paid attention in health.

But I had never seen a first aid kit for the spirit
or heard the word "trauma" to describe

the way I'd hide, slide through the days unseen
or scream into the pillows
at the bottom of my closet
door closed even though no one was home.
Rape wounds deeply, splits open
your core with shrapnel.
The stench of the injury attracts maggots
which hatch into clouds of doubt and self-loathing
the dirt you feel inside you nourishes
anxiety, depression, and shame
poisoning your blood, festering
in your brain until you will do anything to stop
feeling the darkness rising within
anything
to stop feeling—

untreated pain
is a cancer of the soul
that can kill you

Salinger and me

I never thought of killing myself
not on purpose, though I was in grave danger
of a stupid accident, riding sorrow's hamster wheel
living with a popsicle, momsicle, sisicle,
all of us frozen in confusion
me tongueless but alive

When I was little I loved *Bread and Jam for Frances*
the book about a fussy badger
who seemed quite sensible to me.
The author, Russell Hoban, was a fan of J. D.
Salinger—dude who wrote
The Catcher in the Rye, which is a whole
other story.
Hoban said this gobsmacking thing
about Salinger, called him "a man without eyelids"
the line always stuck with me

I was a girl without eyelids that year;
I couldn't blink
I. saw. everything. all. the. time.

my eyes raining constantly from all the seeings,
my throat dry from lack of use
Salinger was a mess, another World War II vet
who came home with nasty memories
shoved into his head
he and my dad would have made great pals
they would have cried and fought and punched
the walls and each other when the lid came off.

We tiptoed, terrified, for years, afraid
my father would kill himself, once and for all,
but he held on, like Salinger, and showed me
that holding on was worth it.

speaking in tongues

When I was a little girl, a friend and her family
moved to the Netherlands and she had to learn
Dutch. I asked if the cows
and the chickens spoke Dutch, too.

Then my brain grew and my mouth grew hungry
for languages—I studied French and German,
tried to read a Russian dictionary.
Exchange students
roamed the halls with their mysteries,
circling in orbits
around Mr. P., my French teacher,
the only one who always smiled
at screwed-up kids like me
and looked us in the eye, like he cared
cuz he did

one afternoon Mr. P. asked me why
I hadn't joined the International Club
he said I'd like it

*(answer: because joining clubs meant being with
people I didn't know, which scared me, and I had
to do that for classes, which is why I forgot to go to
them a lot, but there was no way I was going to do
something that stupid in my free time, no way)*

I told him I was kinda busy
but I'd think about it

locker up

Sound of slamming lockers triggers
me with the spread of metal
across my tongue
as if someone pushed my face
into the steel soldiers lined against the wall,
patiently holding our books, our lunch,
decomposing bananas
and an army of fruit flies,
the combination to open sesame
always slipping past
spin the dial again until it opens, crouch
head in the dark, act
like I'm looking for something important
crowd swelling, banging riot
in the unwatched spaces
me worrying my stack of books
like I can't hear the conversations around me
about some girl who was crying
at the back of the bus,
potato chips and retainers and tryouts,
football players

shoving jockstraps in the faces of girls
no one will defend, essays, big tits and small
dicks,
National Honor Society infighting, drama,
so much drama
I thought I was the only person this alone,
too afraid to lift my head to check, *can rats get
in our lockers did I leave that book at home how much
longer do I have to stay and pretend to pray to this
empty altar, when will the bell release me so I can flip
the page of this script to the shoulder-slumping eter-
nal sigh of time to go to class again*
This is life with your head
inside the jaws
of the beast.

scrawling yawps

when I wasn't stoned
the only thing that helped
me breathe
was opening a book
mist enveloping, welcoming
me into the gray space
between ink black and page white
leading me along to the Shire
to start the long trek to Mordor
again
questing for unknowable treasure
the majesty of Tolkien's adventures
cast a blood spell on me
sap rose from the ground where I was rooted,
filtered through my imagination
it dripped from my fingers as ink-blotted
poetry, scrawled escape recipes
I scribbled,
writing at the speed of life

gauntlet, thrown

My high school was designed by an incarceration
specialist to make the herding, the feeding
and the slaughter proceed as efficiently as possible
that's what we thought,
anyway

the isolated back hallway was an icicle
laid along the school's spine,
I avoided it, cuz it was filled with jocks
but
after detention one day, at the end of ninth grade
tired of wasting my time
going the long way around
I walked down that cold hall,
itching for a fight.

A gym teacher stepped out. The short one
the intimidating one, radiating more energy
than Jean Grey on a cranky day, she pointed
her finger at me and I snapped to attention
and when she said I was a big girl
I said "yes, ma'am"

and when she said I should go out for sports
teams in tenth grade, I said
"yes, ma'am"
because I was terrified of that woman

In the fall, I dove
into the cold, bleaching water
swim practice;
my hair clean for the first time in a year,
I lost myself in underwater meditation
of lap after lap after lap after lap

and that winter I skied
in blue jeans, not caring
that I couldn't afford snow pants,
not giving a shit what other people thought
cuz I was fast, so strong I carved my mark
on the face of the mountain

come spring, I threw shot put and sucked
at throwing discus, but I began myself again
stopped smoking
started chipping away at my concrete cage
went to class every damn day
cuz cutting classes meant I couldn't practice

pulled my grades out of the toilet
stopped phoning in generic answers
and sleeping through class
didn't need to, I slept
finally
at night, too worn out to entertain
the monsters in the closet and under my bed
the nightmares receded into the River Styx
for a while

I experimented with friendships
girls I met on the team,
dusting off the concrete, my fists
uncurled a bit, I stopped
being rabbit-scared
most days

God bless that short gym teacher
for caring enough
to call me out
and hold me up

candy-striped

Mom made me get a job
the summer between
ninth and tenth grades,
between silence
and nervous laughter,
burn and infection.

Anything but babysitting, I said,
and *poof*, I was a candy striper, hospital
volunteer wrapped in a dress with thin stripes
white and tampon-box pink,
I arrived on time five days a week
filled water jugs, delivered flowers
counted hours, fluffed pillows
snuck cigarettes to old folks
in need of a fix. The real lessons
were found in the accidents:
taking a jug of ice
into the wrong room and finding there
a new mother, holding her baby
who'd arrived so broken inside

he couldn't be healed,
wouldn't live long enough to be a bored
teenager, would never blow out
a single birthday candle,
the baby's mother—not much older than me—
she asked for Kleenex and I gave it
and she grabbed my hand
I stood next to her, our fingers entwined
my eyes on the floor
felt wrong to look at her
or the baby
so we held hands
and the ice in the pitcher melted slow
to give them more time.

Another day I took files to the morgue
because computers were still waiting
to be invented. The restless dead hungry
to come back to life, that's what it smelled like
down there, chemicals and meat. Dead-guy hand
on the edge of a table freaked me out
so much that when one of the not-dead guys—
a junior assistant lab rat or something—
asked me for my number, I gave it to him

without thinking
then sprinted for the surface.

He called me. A movie on the first date,
garlic pizza on the second;
movies and pizza was just my speed
slow, turtle-paced, with dumb jokes
and eventually a little kissing
until in the front seat of his car
he pushed my head into his crotch
frantic-fumbling with his belt buckle;
I escaped and avoided
the morgue after that.

ignorance

We didn't get our textbooks in health
in tenth grade until the cold stripped
the trees in late November
cuz the school board ordered the books
to be gutted, they demanded that the sex
chapters be surgically removed
so explanations of the menstrual cycle
and pics of diseased penises
wouldn't send us into frenzied orgies
in the halls or cause us to drop out
so we could do the sex all day.
The school board barred
as much practical education
as they could. Maybe they
just really liked babies and wanted us
to start breeding as soon as possible.

chronological cartography

1. I clawed my way through ninth grade breath by breath, second by second. Kids living in war zones should get extra credit just for showing up to school. The fact that my parents didn't see how messed up I was, and how stoned I stayed to avoid dealing with what messed me up, proved they were fighting hard battles of their own. Dad was hanging on by a thread, but Mom was a warrior. She kept us alive and made sure we had a place to live—two incredible accomplishments, when you think about it. But I didn't think about it, not then. I focused on breathing in, breathing out, then breathing in again.

2. Sophomore year, I tried to be a student, minute by minute. Sometimes hour by hour. My X-kid friends were mad cuz I wouldn't party with them anymore. But I made friends with a girl who swam with me and she was good at discus and I threw the shot put, which landed me with the nickname Moose. I joined the International Club and went to

meetings, and Mr. P. was right—I liked it. My guidance counselor was not impressed with my progress; he shook his finger in my face and yelled at me and said if I didn't get my act together, I'd wind up in jail.

3. By eleventh grade, living hour by hour was habit and every once in a while I could see a little further ahead. I remembered to return library books. I got a job and wasn't fired. Some of my friends' parents didn't like me; they could smell the desperation, the faint whiff of disaster that clung to my clothes. Whatever. I branched into the nonfiction section of the library and read about Russian history and Japanese etiquette. I wrote down important things on a calendar. I watched the musical and went to a couple basketball games, just for fun.

cardboard boxes

I visited kin in the mountains
late in high school, pinned
down in a small town; no car, no cable TV
(internet hadn't been invented, or gaming—hell,
they barely had lights)
our choices were simple: weed, beer, or grain
alcohol mixed
with pink Kool-Aid by spotty boys eager for sex,
sad little puppies living in crumbling houses
or decomposing trailers with pregnant girls from
their algebra class
toddlers sleeping on towels on the floor,
the stench of diapers choking the dogs.

Poor kids get snatched by the real world
at seven, eight, nine years old, dragged
onto the front porch of adulthood, forced
to figure it out on their own
rarely making old bones,
a few will live to see their grandchildren chewed

up by the same machinery
then buried in cardboard boxes
I wanted a coffin made of wood
from trees not yet planted
my appetite for time was growing.

peanut butter chews

the peanut butter chews at my high school,
legendary food of the gods, were simple:
corn syrup, cornflakes, peanut butter, and sugar
mixed, plopped, and baked by badass
cafeteria ladies who understood everything

by eleventh grade, I'd shape-shifted
from a lost stoner dirtbag
to a jock who hung out with exchange students
wrote poetry for the literary magazine
and had a small group of nerdy, funny,
sweet friends to sit with at lunch

my *I'm fine!* mask fit snugly
I only took it off at home,
but when I shared peanut butter chews
with those friends
sometimes I forgot I was wearing it
I studied hard to keep up with them, we listened
to each other and to the same music
we ate a lot of peanut butter chews

the slant of light in the cafeteria
illuminated possibilities

I was smart enough not to tempt fate
by dating any of the guys in that group
I went out with a dude from a different school
who knew me before IT happened, a boy
who loved arguing politics and religion
as much as I did, one of the good guys.

Home was still hellish, afire
with the painful realization
that no matter how much I loved my parents
my love could not fix them

in the mythological universe of high school
cafeteria ladies are the Norns
taking our measure with a glance
seeing whom Fate would cut down early
and who needed an extra peanut butter chew
for free

I could only fix myself

high diving

Once upon a time, this fractured girl
wanted to fly
but was sore-afraid.

I watched teammates leap
off the high dive, flip
themselves into hawks
they called my name
but I chained myself in the far lane
pacing back and forth in the water
churning a wake of frustration,
still
every second stroke as I lifted my mouth
out of the water
to breathe
I opened my eyes to watch the hawks
spear the air

At meets, the diving took place in
the middle of the competition
swimmers turtled in towels on the deck

idle-watching, licking magic sugar powders
with cat tongues, as the divers flew
landing with a splash or a ripple

Once, a friend clipped her wings
on the way down, smashed
her head on the board
before she fell onto the surface
of the water,
they pulled her out, dazed and confused
scrubbed her blood off the board
my friend limped, but flew
a few weeks later, throwing herself
into the air, spinning
spearing
bruising the water
and getting up to try again

every second stroke as I lifted my mouth
out of the water
to breathe
I opened my eyes to watch
until one day my fins
began to grow feathers

germination

idea cracked the seed's shell
skull's cell
burrowed through the muck
surrounding my self-measured casket
clawed blindly toward light

slowly
I can't stand this
bled
into *I can't stay here*
trickled
through *I should leave*
swelled into
I want to leave
rose into a tidal wave
of *I'm going*

riding the undertow

My parents let me apply to be a foreign
exchange student
confident that I'd be rejected
but wanting me to dream
because dreaming was a tradition
at my house, we dreamed
about vacations and adventures, we dreamed
about being other people in different worlds
dreaming was our lifeboat in rough waters

the letter from the exchange program arrived
at the end of my junior year
they accepted me!
I would spend a year and a bit
(thirteen months: delicious, bewitching number)
living on a pig farm in Denmark
fluttering my untested wings

I teetered on the edge of the nest

my mother spelled out the bad news slowly
each word a hammer

because, you see, there was no money
they never thought I would make it so far
but they didn't want to discourage my dream
dreaming never hurt, right?

Two days of tearful negotiation, isolation
rage rattled my mind's cage in search of a solution
forty-eight hours of me standing my ground
relentless, unswayed, I planted my flag
firmly in a hand-forged reality,
if I took all of the money I'd earned
and saved for college
and my grandmother chipped in the difference
of a few hundred dollars
it would work

they talked to each other through the night
my parents did, no longer a question of cash
they weighed the cost of sending
sixteen-year-old
me
overseas to a family they'd never met
they weighed that against the dark tide
always trying to pull us under

we didn't have many books in my house
we had maps of the Adirondack Mountains
and the state of Vermont
because that was the size of our world
in the morning, my mother took the battered
metal globe off my shelf and handed it to me.

"Where the hell is Denmark?" she asked.
"Show me where you're going to live."

the things I carried to Denmark

one suitcase of clothes
a small journal, undersea colors
enough birth control pills
for thirteen months
(thanks, Mom)
I packed my heart beating
rabbit-fast, my eyes
closed and waiting
the small stuffed fish as blue
as the friend who gave it to me
frozen chip on my shoulder
as big as Lake Ontario
backbone a flagpole
nerves thrumming like a scrum
of hummingbirds aloft
the cost of saying goodbye hidden
next to my scars deep in the forest
at the bottom of my gut
I packed my freckled skin, rolled
and tucked between my shinbones
I'd take it out the first night

I arrived, stretch it carefully,
that map of me,
let it rest in the moonlight
on the floor of my bedroom
a baker's dozen of months
so I could roam skinless in the hidden
liminal sliver of fortune granted
by the gambling gods who rolled
their dice in my name.

Around my neck I wore
the Saint Christopher's medal
given by the boy I loved
to keep me safe

it worked.

hvordan det begyndt /
how it started

I left my family behind at the Syracuse airport
flew to NYC, then Hamburg, in Germany
ate a weird pizza with corn on it,
boarded a train for Denmark, didn't sleep
for nearly two nights and two days, didn't want
to miss anything

we were thirty-nine half-growns
from all over the world
gathered in a village near the childhood home
of the writer Hans Christian Andersen
Danish is a tricky language, so we had a month
of instruction to learn how to swallow
Danish vowels
and muffle its marshmallowed consonants
how to say "thank you" / tak
"I don't understand" / jeg forstår ikke
"my name is Laurie" / jeg hedder Laurie
"the bread tastes delicious—may I have another
piece?" / brødet smager læggert—må jeg bede
om et styk til?

friendships were formed fast and hard
like at summer camp, but with better food
and lots more freedom
we walked to the village to buy stamps
and chocolate
sang through the late sunshine
on the endless summer nights

one day we rowed a Viking ship onto the sea
till the land dropped out of sight
we rested our oars, hoisted the sail
compared blisters and dozed
as the breeze rocked us
back and forth, back and forth in our cradle
I unscrewed the top of my head
and rinsed out my brainpan
with salt water from the North Sea
and so began my next life

longitude meets latitude

Mor/Mom, Far/Dad, and Nanna, my Danish sister
picked me up at the language school, we greeted
each other with formal hellos,
like an epic blind date
rode the ferry from one island to another and
drove to the farm
where I had a small room tucked under the eaves
with a window that faced the sunset

the farm's rhythm wound our clocks and flipped
the pages of the calendar

I arrived late summer as the new barn
was being finished
we held a topping-off party to thank
the godspirits in the wood
and celebrate with the carpenters,
Mor made a kransekage
a tower of marzipan cake adorned
with Danish flags and icing
you could hear the wheat growing that afternoon

from where we sat in the garden,
lazy bees buzzing the strawberry bowl,
smells of fresh coffee, cold beer, salt sweat
of the workingmen
and all the while, the fuglekonge/goldcrests
chasing the lowering clouds
reminding us that autumn drew near

We ate our meals together
at the kitchen table, my place
was on the bench across from Mor
and next to my sister
to my left, the door to the vegetable garden
and the fruit trees
our younger brothers taught me the words for food
ymer, smør, hårdkogte æg, ost
and that it was OK to mess up as long as I tried

Far sat at the desk every night after dinner
to record the day's weather and his tasks in a
journal

One Saturday morning, our aunt and uncle
joined us after breakfast

for an important family meeting. I listened deep,
scrambling through my dictionary
when confused, the problem was dire:
rats in the barn were eating everything in sight.
I was so excited because I had learned
enough to be in on the action,
to contribute!
I looked up a few words, cleared my throat
and explained that in America,
when rats got into the grain,
we poisoned them,
but you had to be careful to get rid of the bodies
so they didn't rot

Dead silence
followed by everyone politely pretending
that I had ceased to exist

Months later,
when I could actually understand and speak
I brought up that awkward moment
and asked where I had gone wrong.
Turns out there were no rats in the barn,
they'd been planning
our grandmother's birthday party

and were shocked to hear that in America
we used poison
on such occasions,
we laughed so hard we near peed our pants

Our house stood at the end of the lane
near a bog brimming with eels
Mor opened the windows every day for fresh air
our house expanded magical
so everyone could fit
the cupboards stacked with second chances
sugar bowl filled with encouragement
our house recentered my universe, I rode my bike
to the bakery, library, soccer field, school
and back, always back to our house
at the end of the lane
longitude, eleventh meridian east, built of brick
latitude, fifty-fifth parallel north, family-lit

om efteråret / in the autumn

Monday through Friday, I pedaled to school
a bit more than two miles away,
it felt like ten for the first couple weeks
but got easier and faster quick enough

imagine a mash-up of high school's senior year
and the first year of college, but without a prom,
alcohol poisoning, or sports teams,
and not nearly as much drama.
That's where I went to school: at a studenterkursus
where we called our teachers
by their first names and
could knit in class if we wanted, the theory
being that if we could pay attention
as we knit, we might as well be productive

I studied Danish literature,
English literature, geography,
calculus, history, psychology,
and the hardest of all: French
I'd already studied French for four years,
it was easy

back home, but
at oversætte fra dansk til fransk /
shifting into French from Danish
overheated my brain and melted my circuits

we had a mid-morning break each day
when the school provided coffee,
tea, and pastries
(in Denmark Danish pastry is called Viennese
bread / weinerbrød
because the world is lovely-strange)
it was a relief to just study and grow friendships
without the distractions
and social hierarchies I was used to in the States

once I got used to the routine and the language
and once they got used to me
the shiny-bright of being the new kid,
the American sideshow
faded; that's when I felt homesick.
One night I stood outside with my sister
talking to her about the bone-ache
for my American family
she pointed to the moon and said
it was shining on them, too

and that helped; she is made of compassion,
my sister

when the harvest was done,
the older of our two brothers
was confirmed in the Lutheran church,
an important rite of passage
Danes take their celebrations seriously;
an enormous tent
was erected outside our house, the Norwegian
relatives arrived plus half the town,
course after course of food was served,
then: the speeches. When you celebrate
a confirmation, wedding, birthday,
or anniversary in Denmark,
there are lots of speeches given, equal
parts teasing, mocking, complimenting,
and appreciating. It's a big deal.
I gave a speech for my brother—
apparently I didn't threaten to poison him
like a barn rat, so that was good.
The final course was served at three a.m.
and the party lasted until dawn.

om vinteren / in the winter

as fields slept under winter's snow
deep in the earth a slow rumble
of strong, unseen hands pushed stones
to the surface
rearranging the landscape

I spoke to my American family in July and
again at Christmas
overseas telephone calls were stupid-expensive,
we wrote letters
on onionskin paper, so thin you could see
through it and cheaper to mail

winter Fridays were my long days
the dawn so late that I rode to school in the dark
and by the time I unchained my bike
in the afternoon for the trip home
the sun had again fallen into the sea
as Christmas approached we slaughtered
and processed
the ducks that Mor raised every year to pay for
presents

I was a semi-vegetarian when I left the USA
I got over it in a hurry living on the farm

Scandinavians understand winter, they respect
the long dark
we decorated the Christmas tree with paper stars
and tiny candles
on Christmas Eve, Far carefully lit the wicks
and we all held hands,
dance-walking around the glowing, flickering tree
we sang carols
in a moment light-frozen for all time

I stopped thinking in English somewhen
in that winter
Danish filled my sleep and my waking, cascading
from my mouth like a strong river
victorious after destroying a dam

om foråret / in the spring

come spring, we helped in the fields, burning
off crop stubble and picking the head-sized stones
heaved up through the dirt.
Far frowned at the weather,
consulted his journals, and finally planted,
then frowned at the ground until the green
leapt out

The Three Mile Island nuclear plant outside
Harrisburg, PA malfunctioned
and melted a little in late March,
for a while the experts thought it would blow up
we saw a map on the news that showed
the potential radioactive plume
reaching all the way to Central New York
to kill my family
Mor hugged me as I sobbed, but a few days later,
the plant's meltdown was under control
and the danger passed
then my grandfather died

my bone-ache returned with a vengeance
his death allowed for the third and final
phone call home, I cried
with my father, who was crying thousands
of miles away.
Grandpa wanted all of us grandchildren to see
him in his coffin to learn that death
is to be accepted,
not feared
but if I went back for the funeral,
we couldn't afford the ticket
that would return me to Denmark
for my last three months
so Daddy told me to stay
He sent me photos of his dead father,
bedded in a white funeral box
Grandpa looked surprised,
like when an always-late bus arrives early
after we cleared the stones from the field
that spring
I took to riding my bike down new roads
wandering far

rødgrød med fløde på

Danish reminds me of gargling
with mashed potatoes
forty different vowel sounds
and consonants that melt like soft cheese
a sentence in Danish can sound
like an aimless hum
but the curse words roll like thunder

our neighbors, massive farmers
with granite hands and red faces
liked to tease me by asking me to say rødgrød
med fløde på
which translates to "berry porridge with cream"
if you say it right, it sounds like you're choking
on a furball
I said it wrong for months

other words were easier to pronounce,
but took longer to understand
hygge (now making its way into English)
translates as "cozy"

but is much, much more; hygge
is sitting on a dark winter's night
with friends or family, the room candlelit,
everyone knitting or crocheting
sipping coffee or beer, eating pastry or smørrebrød
talking, talking, listening, talking, enjoying
the pleasure of kindred spirits with the winds
howling outside

tak means "thanks," but that's like saying
Mount Everest is a hill
Danes express gratitude sincerely,
reflexively, constantly
thanking their parents for every meal,
thanking teachers for help, friends
for last night's party,
the butcher for a good cut of meat
tusind tak / "a thousand thanks" is the variation
that I like most
it comes closest to expressing my boundless
gratitude to min danske familie

When summer breezed back in, I finally
conquered rødgrød med fløde på
to the farmers' delight, they shared the phrase's

deeper meaning, rooted
when they were boys carved of bone and sinew,
simmering with rage
because Denmark was occupied by Hitler's army
those farmer boys fought back, sabotaging and
harassing the Nazis
the Germans tried to infiltrate their resistance
when someone was suspected of being a German
spy, the farmer boys
asked him to say rødgrød med fløde på
if he didn't pronounce it right, it was the last thing
he ever said.

In Denmark, in Scandinavia, across Europe
memories of World War II ache like a scar
does when the weather changes or a storm
draws near
old countries are riddled with battle wounds
that split open, bleed, and cause new pain
if not cared for,
just like us

scars may look stronger than unwounded skin,
but they're not
once broken, we're easily hurt again, or worse

the temptation is to hide behind shields,
play defense, drown ourselves in sorrow
or drug our way to haunted oblivion
until death erases hope

My home in Denmark taught me how to speak
again, how to reinterpret darkness and light,
strength and softness
it offered me the chance to reorient my compass
redefine my true north
and start over

bridging

to go straight from our Danish homes
back to our families of origin
would have screwed everybody up
we needed a breather
a break

they sent us to Lejre,
half an hour from Copenhagen
to an Iron Age archaeological center
where researchers were puzzling out
how ancient Danes
crossed bogs and swamps
three thousand years earlier
they needed young, strong bodies not afraid of work
we thirty-nine half-growns from all over the world
had to build a bridge

we
used axes to hew logs for the frame
tied fat bundles of saplings and green branches
for the foundation, dumped them in the water
like offerings to the bog

we ate meat roasted over the open fire
devoured bread, yogurt, and cheese
slept on a thin layer of straw in a giant tent
all of us together, drifting deep and dreamless
waking achy, grabbing our tools
chopping, carving, cursing
wrangling, working, wearing
ourselves out of our skins
and into the harnessed spirit
of samarbejde/cooperation
in which the melding of individual energies
far exceeds the sum of the parts

eventually we fed the hungry bog enough wood
that our bridge broke the water's surface
like the back of a rising horse
we shoveled dirt to fill the interstitial spaces
formed a line to pass big rocks
hand to hand
body to body
building upon our foundation with weight, sweat,
and strength
added more dirt to make the walking easy
the researchers led an oxen team across our bridge

to test our work
and declared our bridge worthy

we raised our glasses and axes in salute
feasted
showered in cold water
and prepared for our next crossing

commence reentry sequence

space capsule
screaming through the atmosphere
heat shield melting, parachutes out,
I landed back in the USA
after thirteen lifetimes,
I mean, months
away

English didn't fit right in my mouth
det var meget nemmere at tale dansk,
mere behagelig
jeg glemte oversættninger, hvordan man siger
agurker/cucumbers eller erindringer/memories
men da jeg genfornede
med min americanske familie
the important words finally came back

after much hugging and happy tears
we sat close together on the couch, my mother
constantly tucking a stubborn lock of hair
behind my ear
my father's heavy hand patting my shoulder

my sister sitting on the floor,
leaning against my knee
you don't get many perfect moments in life
our reunion was one of them

next morning, I rode my bike
to the high school, July-flying through the miles
didn't have to stand on the pedals
up the long, steep hill
my thighs steel-reinforced
after a year of riding overseas

Summer-break school mostly empty,
the halls smelled the same
goose-bumpy
in the main office I explained
my mission and the secretary
opened a drawer, pulled the file
with my name on it
my permanent record
removed my diploma and almost
gave it to me, but paused
to add the grave pomp
called for by the circumstance,
she shook my hand

"Congratulations," she said, formally.
"You have graduated."

And so began the next chapter
in a familiar place where everything was different
a well-cloaked alien, I heard my old world
filtered through Nordsøens vand / North Sea water
and saw it in the light of dansk solskin /
Danish sunshine

separation—AWOL 1

While I was somewhere-the-hell in Denmark,
my American family had moved again
this time to a small house rented
from a guy who made it clear
that if my mother slept with him,
he'd cut us a deal.
(Instead she worked overtime.)

I came home stronger
taller
wounds tended and scarred over

But my parents had started drinking
every morning by eight, instead of waiting
for the sunset,
Daddy drank to blur
the steel edge of his failures.
Mommy drank to keep
from killing him. She went to work
after gargling and spitting.

Daddy worked a little,
walked a lot on the towpath
crowded with ghosts. Wrote poetry,
cried, contemplating suicide
trying to ride out the tide of despair
and keep breathing.

One day I came home
to the sound of a hammer
on metal. My mother
roared all the curse words
she'd once scrubbed out of my mouth
with a bar of Ivory soap.

I crept to the door of my parents'
bedroom, afraid of the bloody body
certain to be staining the floor.

Mommy was alone, beating
the piss out of their bed frame
with a sixteen-ounce hammer.

She looked up,
narrowed her eyes

"Time for separate beds," she snarled,
dragon smoke curling out of her mouth.
"He's gone to Boston for a while."

WHAM! She beat a bolt on the bed frame.
"A long while." *WHAM, WHAM!*

"Hamburger Helper for dinner," she added.
"Start browning the meat."

reunion—AWOL 2

Dad came home nine months
later. He looked better, didn't drink
until four p.m., and only screamed
in his sleep a couple nights a week.

I'm still convinced he ran off
with a woman, but whatever.
Mom let him back in the door.
The Church did, too. The Church
that had cast him out, her broken son,
gave back his dignity, his calling
and his God after six years in the wilderness

We moved again after his prodigal return
this time to a rural church filled
with farmers, teachers, and nurses.
I slept that first winter on the floor
under the dining room table
because my bedroom didn't have heat
or insulation. A glass of water left there

overnight was ice come morning,
from Thanksgiving till after Easter.

I found work milking cows.
Dad found some peace mending hearts.
Our mother found a tumor in her left breast.
She never put their beds back together.

hitchhiking with my father

Driving with Daddy was risky,
cuz he drove
with one foot on the accelerator
and the other on the brake, confident
of his superior reflexes
and the power of his smile.

When I was two, he drove us
all the way to Florida, me roaming
in the back of the station wagon untethered,
waving to horrified strangers
for fifteen hundred fraught miles.

We survived that trip unscathed.
Others, not so much; he'd crash into a ditch
or park on a highway late at night
traffic thundering inches away
while my parents fought
about who should take the wheel.

I loved my dad,
but he was a shitty driver
and the booze sure didn't help.

After high school, we stopped talking, it hurt
so much to love my father that I prayed
for a heart of stone,
like God gave Pharaoh.
The years of praying for him to be healed
hadn't worked; he kept messing up,
breaking down, throwing our lives out of orbit,
but I still thought of God
as a kind of Cranky Dad who might
consider my plea if I asked politely.

One afternoon, my father found me in tears—
I'd missed the bus and was going to be fired.
I needed that job cuz no college
would have me back then.
Daddy's face softened, for a moment
he was the father who'd take us out of school
on a whim to go mountain climbing

or buy ice cream for every kid on the block.

"You're too young
to hitchhike alone," he said.
"I'll go with you, make sure you're safe."

strawberry-blonde fairy tales

My mother, my sister, and I got up at five
on that July morning,
three women with nothing in common
save blood, disappointment, and the inherited,
trauma-fed ability
to stay silent in every situation,
we united in the need for a televised dream
live, from London

A multigenerational fantasy, the about-to-be-
princess,
sewn into confectionary silk taffeta, rode
in a glass bubble pulled by white horses,
a virgin paraded for the masses, Madonna
of diamonds and luck. Ten thousand pearls hung
from the dress, the fruit of relentless
irritation, the day's slippery portent of doom
though, in the manner of crowds, no one noticed.

Lady Diana Spencer was three months older
than me,
raised on the same fairy tales and lies.

My mother, my sister, and I ate strawberries,
sprinkled with sugar, swimming in cream,
as we cooed like doves watching the fantasy
come to life. I'd long ago selected myself
as Prince Andrew's bride,
cuz Charles was too much work.
My sister reserved herself for Prince Edward,
and our mother looked forward to tea
with the Queen.
Cinderella's country cousins, we giggled,
our parsonage a small island
in whispering fields of corn.

That morning gave me the only peek
I ever had inside my mother's imagination,
and thus planted me eternally on #TeamDiana
in the hopes I'd be allowed to visit again.

But recessionals play in a minor key;
the princess pricked her finger on a spindle,
was shattered by mirrors, cursed by fairies,
banished from the kingdom, and hunted
down by dogs. Trolls hide under bridges
and that's where she died.

Sixteen years after the wedding
I woke in the darkness for the funeral.
My mother self-exiled to Florida
sister long lost to us both, I watched alone,
no strawberries, no sugar, no cream,
sipped coffee as black horses pulled the coffin
through the weeping city.

Rich people scorn the way the poor
buy lottery tickets,
but what would you pay for an hour
of untainted hope, of happiness unfettered?

If the ticket had my mother's name on it
I'd dance across minefields for the chance.

manure

Living on a pig farm did not motivate
me to go to college
not picking stones from the fields
nor burning off crop stubble
nor penning up ducks trying to escape
nor plucking their feathers after slaughter
so they could be served at Christmas.

Working on a dairy farm didn't motivate
me, either. I liked the sound of slow-breathing
cows, bruises from kicking hooves
shoveling manure, herding the girls
in from the green, chased by a bull once
I sprinted and slid to safety
under an electric fence,
freezing, sweating, muscle-burning work
made me grateful
I wasn't stuck inside.

No, it was my job in hell,
I mean, at the mall, selling shirts

folding sweaters, moldering into a minimum-
wage service clone, clothing store sorter
of boxes of socks of urgent priority, avoider
of the manager, my mom, momager of a different
kind, she had high hopes for me,
business school for sure,
then the chance to follow in her footsteps
and be every bit as miserable as she,
circling from mall to television set,
television set to the mall.

For years I thought that was her plan
but recently I've begun to doubt it,
remembering her proud satisfaction
when I made a better life for myself.
I think that giving me the most boring job
in the history of the world
was my mom's way of loving me.

lazer focused

I woke up at three thirty a.m.,
was in the barn milking by four,
headed home for a long shower,
then drove to school
Onondaga Community College,
home of the Lazers,
went to all my classes and stayed awake,
asked questions, did my homework, studied hard
and always sat in the front row.
When you are shoveling
cow poop to pay your tuition,
you want to get your money's worth, every dime.

Some people grow up knowing what they want
to do: they color inside the lines,
study at the right school,
check off the boxes, and
in the end
they are handed the grown-up life
they've dreamed of.

That's mostly bullshit, for the record.

Trying to figure out what you want to do,
who you want to be, is messy as hell; the best
anyone can hope for is to figure out
the next step.

For me the first step was to try college,
then a university, if I could get a scholarship,
to study translation: the art, science, and magic
of distilling meaning from one language
to another

but complications ensued
and the plot twisted, hard.

drawn and quartered

At community college we had a professor
sweet and fangless
he was known as "the widow"
raising nine kids on his own.

Cancer ate most of his wife
but her pregnant womb
was the fortress resisting the final bite
long enough to breathe
life into their phoenix child,
who was born in bitter grace.

That professor taught anatomy
breastbone connected
to ribs, pelvis to spine
and so on
he waxed rhapsodic about the form
of the female leg. Drew one on the board,
a small, high-arched foot wearing
a stripper-pole stiletto. The angle
of the heel tightening
the gastrocnemius muscle

of the calf, he traced the action,
contraction of muscles, drawing,
climbing the leg's ladder until he reached
his favorite part: the gluteus maximus.
My sweet, fangless professor drew
big, bulbous buttocks
like heavy, low-hanging fruit
he patted them fondly, wanting
to take a bite, he told us
that this sweet curve of ass
was why Barbie dolls' feet
were formed for shoes
with ridiculous heels
plastic foot-binding
for girl children,
objectification
served with mother's milk

He never fondled, never hit
on any of us students, that old man,
but still
we left his class
feeling a little dirty.

calving iceberg

and then it was time to say goodbye
again
we packed the station wagon
for my last leaving, for the predawn trip
to Georgetown; me, my sister
Daddy and Mom,
all of us knowing
none of us saying
that I'd never live in their house again
though I'd visit when I could
the drive to D.C. hurt
the unpacking of my suitcase
positioning my alarm-clock radio
gooseneck study lamp
hot-air popcorn popper
everything hurt
as a transfer student I had a single,
no roommate to break the suffocating
silences, the awkward fumbling
for tissues, Daddy making jokes
sprinkled with bad puns so we could groan
out loud and pretend to laugh

I had no microwave or fridge or TV
but I had my dictionaries
and a phone for local calls
and envelopes with stamps
my mother cried all day long
I tried not to look at her because
it hurt
it all hurt so much
the necessary, impossible goodbye
that had suddenly, in slow motion, arrived
weakening our knees
we leaned on each other
putting my T-shirts in the drawer
hanging up my towel
unwrapping a bar of soap
opening the new toothbrush
sharpening the pencils and placing them tip up
in a plastic cup next to my typewriter
Mommy brought extra bottles of Wite-Out
cuz she knew how many mistakes I'd make
they had a six-hour drive home
so we didn't have time for dinner
we limped down the stairs
down the stairs we limped
cuz it hurt

it still hurts
my father and my sister poured
the wet ocean of my mother into the car
buckled her in, then limped to their own doors
the melting begins at the waterline
as young icebergs prepare to calve from glaciers
the breaking off is always preceded by a rift
rarely seen by outside eyes
but felt inside the heart of the ice
the eruption, the split makes a noise
heard for miles across oceans
of salt water and time
the ripples are still washing ashore

sweet-and-sour tea

I went shopping with a new sorta-friend
my first semester at Georgetown, aliens
warily circling each other, sniffing for clues,
both of us desperate and lonely
cuz she was British boarding schools
and flying first class while I was a hillbilly
who worked on farms, chopped wood,
shoveled manure, and milked cows.
But we smelled some possibility,
so she led, I followed
and after hours of watching her buy things
(I'd never seen someone my age with a credit card)
she announced we should have a proper
English tea, her treat,
which sounded good to me.

We floated into a restaurant, perched
on Cinderella couches, spread cloth napkins (!)
on our laps, and she ordered tiny sandwiches and
a high-class blend that came with its own pedigree
I asked for plain tea, regular folks' tea,

the waitress asked me, "Cream or lemon?"
and I said, "Both."

It was the first cup of tea of my entire life.

Tiny, crustless sandwiches arrived
you needed two to make a mouthful
and the waitress poured our tea
into skin-thin china cups
we spooned in heaps of melting honey
added thick cream, already heated
and stirred silver spoons in an arpeggio
of satisfaction, *tink, tink, tink*
I was a glowing, sparkly unicorn
in love with a life that suddenly included
tea and cute sandwiches. I picked up the slice
of lemon and I squuuuuuuuuueeeeeezed
it into my dream cup

It curdled instantly, it damn
near turned into cottage cheese

for a horrified moment
we both stared in my cup
I waited,

praying for a friendly laugh to bridge
her world and mine, the way I'd laugh
sweetly
if she ever tried to milk a cow
and screwed up, which she would,
cuz it's hard, but my laugh
would ring warm like a copper bell
and I'd help her

She snorted, her lip curled.
Scorn dripped from her chin
and burned holes in the tablecloth
torching any hope we could be friends.

Most relationships come with expiration dates
just like milk and bread. Some go sour
before you can taste them.

offending professors

Young flesh perfumed with trust
smells like fresh meat
to stalking professors
dreaming of the feast
it happened to me
twice

One: at community college, my health professor
invited me to celebrate the A+ he gave
me for a paper I wrote about LSD
he said we could drink wine at a motel, his treat
he said we would have awesome sex at the motel
he said his wife was totally cool
with him fucking students at motels
when I declined the offer
and tried to leave, he chased me around the desk
he blocked the exit
bullying me to at least make out with him
I didn't

Two: at Georgetown University,
my department head

invited me into his office to discuss my need
for a special scholarship to study in Peru.
To be able to translate Spanish, I'd need to live
in a country where it was spoken
I brought notes to the meeting, all my pla—
he lifted his hand to interrupt me
the department head said that we had been lovers
centuries earlier
we'd been Aztecs, had sex in the jungle
he said that we were cosmic soul mates
and needed to have sex again, unite our bodies—
I walked out before the ritual chase
around the desk

Shielded by ivy curtains, tenured lions
force their prey to sprint from the water hole
in any direction that seems safe
even if it takes them far afield from their goals
he didn't give me that scholarship
I never studied in Peru
never studied in any country
where Spanish is spoken
never became a translator
unless telling stories counts

grinding it out

I sailed to Georgetown University on a rowboat
kept afloat by student loans and
working twenty-five hours a week
water rushed in the holes at the bottom
so I bailed day and night,
just fast enough to stay above water
worked as a lifeguard,
stayed in D.C. every summer
rented a cot in a hallway, stored my clothes under it
then shared a small house with five people who
hated each other
good times
sold *Time Life* books over the phone, a gross job
but they let me call my grandmother every day
and talk to her for an hour *for free,*
instead of the thirty dollars
that daytime calls to Florida cost back then
when minimum wage was $3.35 an hour
you better believe I worked hard for them,
I loved my nana
at college I skipped breakfast, ate an apple

and granola bar for lunch
and feasted at dinner; *thank you, meal plan buffet*
at Georgetown I stewed my brain
in German and Spanish
when Peru was taken off the table
cuz of the predatory department head
I earned a degree in linguistics, charting
the transformation of languages
over time, vowels waltzing, consonantly flirting
words flinging open windows to the past
I avoided studying literature and writing class
married the sweetest guy I met there
who loved overseas adventures and politics
and looked really good in shining armor
the marriage didn't work; we were way too young,
but he is still my dear friend

I loved the ancient magnolia tree
that grew next to the library
shading anxious students, perfuming the air
inviting us to stand in her cool shade
and breathe in: inspire, breathe out: expire,
catch hold of our trueselves,
sew them tight to our shadows

before the pressure of performing blew us all away
magnolia leaves are huge, waxy,
shaped like rowboats
the perfect escape for a mouse
or a small-feeling person
I didn't need one, not anymore
I was in way over my head at Georgetown
but at least I knew how to swim

scratching my throat with a pen

After college, our wedding, after the babies came,
we were so broke I had to get a night job
cuz we couldn't afford child care:
I became a reporter
perfect work in the dark for a shy child
beginning to clear her throat

Sewer board meetings—oh, the glamour!
and the stench of government corruption,
small-stage culture wars on school boards,
union officials who lied to me, straight-faced
just like the mom who said her kid cut
up his mouth on glass shards in his cereal
total bullshit, she later confessed
she just wanted attention and some cash

I asked questions, took notes,
wrote, wrote, wrote, wrote, wrote, wrote
revised, sniffed out lies, unburied
the lede, factual recitations
my specialty, I inquired

as required
accidentally acquiring
a calling to listen very carefully
and try to write the truth

cave painting

I'd been scribbling ever since
Mrs. Sheedy-Shea taught me haiku:
stories, poems, fairy tales, mysteries,
gothic nightmares
and, occasionally, happy endings

when I had babies I tried to write for them, too,
I sucked
but persisted, resisting the temptation to quit

I wrote picture books
that sucked so bad
they were rejected over and over and over again
but I persisted, enlisting new friends
all of us thirsting to write and be read

I pounded out novels and nonfiction,
major suckage, constantly, appropriately rejected
I freaking persisted, insisting I could figure
it out

The stories, the words, the phrases
coming out of the mists persisted,
even when I wanted
to pack it in, give it up, and get out.
My existence insisted
on listening to the voices in my head distantly
cheering my ambition

I tried a new thing—revision—
and persisted, dismissing my doubts, risking
my pride

demystifying a process
that consisted of untwisting the trysting words
in my brainpan and convincing them
to behave
inspiration and craft slowly melding
into this, the consistent beat of my words
against the drum

if it please the court

the courthouse reporter was out sick one day
so they sent me in his place, the defendant
a plain white guy, late thirties,
kinda small, cheap suit,
good haircut, charged with ugly counts
of sexual assault, plus kidnapping
he looked bored

She went to a party with friends,
hey, nineteen, a good time;
loud music and wine coolers
the night warm enough for the crowd
to dance outside, yeah, he was older
but older guys always showed up
invited or not. After dancing under the stars,
she had to go home, but the girl who drove
there was wasted and she didn't have enough cash
for a cab
so, looking bored, he offered
to drive her home
a gentleman,
on the way he asked if they could stop

at his parents' house for a sec
so he could let out the dog, a puppy
she loved puppies
so she followed him into his parents' house
and found that there was no puppy,
no parents
just a roll of duct tape
and twenty-four hours of torture
as the police recited the details
the rapist yawned

Defense lawyer did his job
by attacking the victim
shouting that she drank, she danced,
she dressed to look good
she wanted it, she followed him
liked it rough
or planned on marriage or extortion
as she cried on the stand, long blonde hair
in front of her face, a curtain for her sanity,
he painted her into a corner with accusations
fantastical but just barely legal
screaming lawyers objected
counter-objected, sustained, upheld
blind justice torn apart by jackals

the jury confused
that young woman shook so hard
I thought the roof would cave in

ever been in a fight?
fists like hammers, punches thrown
rose-red bloom filling the room
as your rage catches fire
an exploding can of spray paint
when you see that red
shit's gonna get real
you're gonna hurt someone
or do something stupid
probably both
I saw that red, as the victim shook
cuz she'd thought she was safe
thought there was a puppy
I saw myself crawling over the seats, leaping
throwing punches, busting knuckles, breaking
a chair over his head, the sweet sound of his teeth
skittering across the floor

my pencil snapped

me, still in my chair, notebook soaked

sweat dripping down my face
judge banged the gavel
BAM!
ended the day early
I stayed till the court emptied and I could breathe
again,

told the story to my editor, who did the right thing
for journalism
by assigning someone else to cover the trial
defense lawyer negotiated a plea bargain,
the rapist
sentenced to some easy time in county jail,
a mild slap on the wrist

Years later, walking in the mall
with my daughters tall and gangly
I saw him again, that rapist
only that time, he didn't look bored
because
he was hunting

how the story found me

An old woman rocks in my subconscious
sending songs, hidden messages, *spor*—
//record scratch//

I dream a lot in Danish
when I wake up from a danskdrøm
I confuse the two languages
until the coffee kicks in,
this morning as I worked on a draft of this poem,
I centered
it on the word *spor*
I said the old woman who wanders
in the woods of my mind
who knits in the rocking chair of my subconscious
she shows me the *spors*,
the hints of what passed this way
when I wasn't paying attention,
and what lies ahead in wait
except the word in English is "footprints,"
or "animal tracks"

the dashes left in snow by a frightened rabbit
punctures made by the chasing wolf

maybe she is future me, that old dame
maybe future me sends my dreams /
mine drømme
to now me, or past me, as warnings/advarsler
or advice/råd, or maybe she's just messing with me
and cackling

my nightmares repeat over and over
until I pay attention, pay my respects
to whatever is eating
at me; one night, just as my oldest
started middle school
I heard a girl sobbing, brokenhearted
I jolted awake and checked on my daughters
convinced that I'd heard one of them, but no,
the crying girl was lost in my head
and she wouldn't let me sleep
because she couldn't speak
and she needed an interpreter
so I started writing in the middle of that night
the stream of unconscious eventually merging

with my waking self, a year of scribbling
mostly before dawn

turns out the mother word is *spor* in Old English,
Germanic, Old Norse, and survives
unchanged in Danish
pops up in modern English as *spoor*
borrowed from Afrikaans in 1823
so I wasn't as trapped between languages
as I thought
and the hour spent swimming
in multilingual etymology
was its own reward

the first publisher I sent *Speak* to rejected it
I never thought anyone would publish the story
let alone read it

I am often distracted, diverted
from my path when I explore old wounds
it's a defensive reaction,
a way to modulate my feelings
and cope with the discomfort,

like telling jokes at a funeral,
not appropriate, but less damaging than gin

too many grown-ups tell kids to follow
their dreams
like that's going to get them somewhere
Auntie Laurie says follow your nightmares instead
cuz when you figure out what's eating you alive
you can slay it

Speak, Draft One, Page One
(from my journal)

FIRST MARKING PERIOD

I'm looking for the key
to open the door
to this story

an overheard motel
room conversation
if they would just turn down the television
I could hear the words clearly,
maybe find the magic
formula.

No outline. Not this time,
just a character on a page,
the stage
spotlighted
and alone
with her fear,
heart open,

unsheltered.
Melinda, age 14.
Trapped in a year with no calendar
pages, just day after day
of 14,
cuz the hands of the clock
in biology class are frozen
at five till three.

two

Polyhymnia

It is my first morning of high school.
I
have seven new notebooks,
a skirt I hate,
and a stomachache.
(opening lines of Speak*)*

I began high school (my fourth school in four
years)
with six polyester skirts, not just one,
all sewn by my grandmother,
who loved me so much
she didn't want me to start
the new school in hand-me-downs,
cuz the rich kids would laugh
she sewed me six skirts
the colors of autumn
so I could wear a brown turtleneck
with all of them. I armored
myself that first day
(two weeks after the boy raped me)
with incantations grandmaternal;

love-sewn skirt, unheard prayers,
a penny in each loafer, I walked to the bus stop
then to the gallows

my first day of ninth grade had no assembly
no "First Ten Lies They Tell You in High School"
no showdown with Mr. Neck
Speak is a novel
rooted in facts, to be sure,
but a story bred with its own DNA
an invasive species growing out of a stump
of a tree hit by lightning
growing from the girl who survived

the overlap of my stories and my life
is a garden courtyard, sky-strung with stars
and scars where planets were torn
from their orbits
the courtyard where that stump grows
is surrounded by stone walls
three miles high, carved
with thousands of locked doors
and secrets that bloom open
in the moonlight

conspiracy

They said if *Speak* sold a couple thousand copies
we'd be lucky, cuz teenagers didn't like to read
I had no expectations or hopes
I never thought it would be published at all

one day a man called me to tell me
I was a finalist
for the National Book Award
confused, I called my editor
who explained that I needed to buy a dress
a fancy one, cuz this was a seriously big deal

country mouse in New York City
I scurried to events, anxious, unsure
tried to blend into the wallpaper
my fellow finalists more comfortable
with the shiny new world that required dresses
or suits, riding in cabs instead of on the subway

student journalists gathered to interview
us, the Fab Five Finalists, onstage:
Walter Dean Myers, *Monster*

Louise Erdrich, *The Birchbark House*
Kimberly Willis Holt, *When Zachary Beaver
Came to Town*
Polly Horvath, *The Trolls*
and me,
the spotlights in our eyes made it hard to see
our interrogators, but the questions were
thoughtful.
When it was over the kids filed out,
and we headed for the door
toward lunch at a posh restaurant
on someone else's dime
but Walter
Walter was deep in conversation
with one of the students,
talking books and Harlem
and other important things
I waited by the door for him

Walter was the first established author I'd met
he welcomed me into the world of books for kids
with joy, wisdom, and grace, he taught
me everything I know about my responsibility
to my readers, starting that day

cuz he didn't go to lunch at all, he waved us off
that young man was filled with questions
and Walter had some answers
and questions of his own
he made the time for a reader
because integrity required it
that's what we're called to do

the award dinner was mad stressful, the chairman
of my publisher's company sat at my table
he'd flown in from Germany for the event
and didn't look happy about it
that made two of us; my dress itched,
my shoes pinched
nervous-thirsty, I drank gallons of water
constantly racing to the bathroom to pee

Walter sat at the table next to mine
throughout the evening, he'd turn
and tell me a joke
point out how glamorous events
like this had nothing to do with the sweat
of writing,
but the desserts were good

when the time came, we enjoyed
Oprah Winfrey's speech
Steve Martin pronounced my name right,
that was impressive,
then the chair of the Young People's Literature jury
approached the podium
she talked about how much kids love to read,
how they found books through family,
friends, librarians,
the people who would read aloud to them. . . .

Walter looked at me and arched an eyebrow
he and I wrote for the kids
who didn't have those people
children with scars
inside and out, kids whose childhoods
disappeared in the rearview mirror
a long time ago
he leaned forward and whispered, "We're screwed"
which made me laugh, we clapped
and cheered for Kimberly
because she wrote a great book, too,
then Walter poured me a glass of wine
first one of the evening but not the last

we toasted each other
we celebrated writing for the kids
the world doesn't want to see

earlier, when the student journalists
interviewed us
one commented about the friendly vibe
of the Fab Five Finalists, asked
"Aren't you supposed to be competitors?"
Walter took the mic and smiled
"No," he said. "Not competitors.
We're coconspirators, and we like it that way."

That was when I knew I was home.

tsunami

tens of thousands speak
words ruffling the surface of the sea
into whitecaps, they whisper
into the shoulder of my sweater
they mail
tweet, cry
direct-message
hand me notes
folded into shards
when no one is watching

sharing memories and befuddlement
broken dreams and sorrow
they struggle in the middle
of the ocean, storms battering
grabbing for sliced life jackets
driftwood
flotsam and jetsam from downed
unfound planes, sunken ships
and other disasters

if they can keep their heads up
they swim for the nearby
Melindas
to help them save
themselves from drowning
in that hungry sea of despair
as they lift up their sisters
and brothers
and those who claim their space
beyond old definitions
they tell their stories
and speak their truth

earthquakes in deep water
send ripples to the surface
that crave the shore
thundering
toward land, sounding
like a freight train
the fatetrain, monsooning,
pulls back the shallows
exposing the bones of ocean
messages in bottles

tossed overboard

Hwæt!
the chorus swells the tidal wave
tsunamis overcoming gravity
knocking down the doors

blowing up

girls and boys tell me, shame-smoked raw
voices, tears waterfalling,
about the time
IT forced its dick
into her mouth
or his mouth
or their mouth
stopped up the breathing
scared shut the screams

the mouth they want
to eat with, smile
with, sing with, paint
with glitter, lip-
stick, and stain
with grape popsicles
or wine from a dark sea, a mouth
to whisper with love, to open
wide and swallow
what love offers, hungry
always for more.

Apologetically bile-gagged,
they tell me
they know they should feel
grateful
because they weren't . . . .
. . . . . .
. . . . should feel
grateful
because they weren't . . . .
"raped"

and they set the word
"raped"
between quotation marks
"   "

feeling somehow wrong
about admitting their pain
knowing that others
hurt differently

I wasn't "raped"
locking the word
into a cage
"   "

filled with legal definitions,

a cage built on quicksand
a shame-forged prison of self-doubt
those marks jail
their truth
behind a false narrative,
an unholy competition
that no one wants to play.

Let the lawyers keep score,
if you must
let the court tally the points
for conviction or against
for six months in the county lockup
six years in the federal pen

Pain won't be contained
by bars or marks
your scars deserve attention, too.

collective

a what? of teens
a wince of teens
mutter of teens
an attitude, a grumble, a grunt
a disenchantment of teenage girls
a confusion of teen boys

when I talk about *Speak* to a class
or an auditorium full of teenagers
there's always that guy
in the back row wearing a jersey
soccer or lacrosse or football
he's a good boy, he asks
the first real question—

"Why was Melinda so upset?
I mean, it wasn't a bad guy with a gun
who dragged her down an alley;
she liked the guy, danced with him,
she kissed him,
so what's the big deal?"

a kiss of boyfriends
a dance of rapists

what's the big deal?
asked at every kind of school
all over the country
curious boys honestly inquiring
their friends squirming

a quest of knights errant
a smirk of dudes

the question is born out of true confusion
no one ever told him the rules of intimacy
or the law, his dad only talks about condoms
with a "don't get her pregnant" warning
his mom says "talk to your father"
so he watches a lot of porn
to get off
to be schooled
porn says her body is territory
begging to be conquered
no conversations required
you take what you want

an occupation of men

those boys taught me
to talk about consent
get real about consequences
respect the room enough
to tell the truth
cuz, lordy lord, they need it

other boys pull me aside for a private
conversation, they say one of their friends,
a girl who was raped
is depressed and cutting and getting high
to forget what happened, they want to help
make it better, they want to kill
the guy who did it
they're trying to be righteous, honorable
but they're not sure how

a vengeance of puppies

some boys talk about being abused by men
of becoming a locker room target
of never using the bathroom in school
not even once in four years

cuz that's a dangerous place
if you're not an alpha running with the right pack

a few became bullies
tired of being teased, beat on,
made to feel small, left out in the cold
they attack the quiet boys
the isolated, who walk in the shadows
some of the bullies are homebred monsters
built by Frankendads, limb by limb
filled with regret and juiced by shame

a retribution of scars

my husband did the math, calculated
I've spoken to more than a million teens
since *Speak* came out, those kids
taught me everything, those girls
showed me a path through the woods

those boys led me
to write *Twisted*,
my song of admiration
to young men paying the price
for their fathers' failures

the collective noun I'm seeking is "curiosity"
we have a curiosity of boys
waiting on the truth
and when their questions
go unanswered
the suffering begins for

an anguish of victims

emergency, in three acts

ACT ONE
Once upon a time, a year or so after *Speak*
was published
a high school in New Jersey invited an author
(guess who)
to speak about a book (you know the one)

Picture this: the author (yep, you guessed right)
takes the stage for the first presentation
and stands in the spotlight
owns the microphone
preaches facts about power
and bodies and sex and violence
speaks up, on fire

INTERMISSION, BUT BRIEF:
One thousand students tumble out
next thousand students roll in
Showtime!

ACT TWO
The author (still me) opens

her mouth, my mouth, but instead of spitting
words,
the fire alarm erupts
silencing me.
It is the only way Principal Principal—
quaking in his shiny black shoes,
either terrified of parents
or guilty as hell—
can think to shut me up

the entire school mingles in the drizzly parking lot
a group of girls gathers
around me quietly, quickly
speaking
of the boys who touch
them in the halls, pull
them under the stairs
rape
whomever they can get drunk enough
on the weekends

the alarm bells keep ringing and ringing and
ringing
but no rescue arrives

ACT THREE

When the screaming alarms are finally silenced

Principal Principal tells me my day

is done

talking about sex

               and rape

                      and bodies

                             and touching

     and consent

and violence

is not appropriate for the children

under his care

because

those things don't ever happen

in his school

librarian on the cusp of courage

"I loved your book," says the librarian
"*Prom*, not *Speak*."

I open my mouth to—

"Course I can't have it in my library," she adds.

I close my mouth

"The main character," she rushes on

I listen

"She's disrespectful to authority,
cuts class, sleeps with her boyfriend . . ."

I wait

"We can't have those kinds of examples on the
shelves."

Bingo

"And by the end of the book?" I ask

"Well . . ." She touches her crucifix.

I wait
thinking of the miles of empty shelves
in the hearts of her students

"Well"—
blinks her doll-blue eyes—
"she does change and grow by the end.
And the prom scenes were fun."

Exactly the opening I was
hoping for
now we can have a
conversation

She drops her eyes to the concrete floor.
"I can't afford to lose my job."
She runs.

inappropriate dictators

A public school superintendent in Florida
proclaimed
"As of September 8, 2017,
no instructional materials (textbooks,
library books, classroom novels,
etc.)"—**THIS "etc." SLAYED ME**—
"purchased and/or used by the school district
shall contain any profanity,
cursing"—**REDUNDANCY IS A SIGN YOU DIDN'T
PAY ATTENTION IN ENGLISH CLASS**—
"or inappropriate subject matter."

**"Inappropriate"
was when I burst
into flames**

*Without Freedom of Thought,
there can be no such Thing as Wisdom;
and no such Thing as publick Liberty,
without Freedom of Speech.
—Benjamin Franklin, 1722*

So many problems could be solved
with just a teeny bit of knowledge
about American government,
the Constitution,
and the function of the Supreme Court, like
in *Board of Education, Island Trees Union Free*
    School District No. 26
v. Pico, 457 US 853, 872 (1982),
when the Supremes memorably sang:

> *Supreme Court precedent*
> *condemns school officials who*
> *remove books "simply because they*
> *dislike the ideas contained in those*
> *books and seek by their removal to*
> *'prescribe what shall be orthodox in*
> *politics, nationalism, religion,*
> *or other matters of opinion.'"*

Censorship is the child of fear
the father of ignorance
and the desperate weapon of fascists
everywhere.

innocence

censoring my books
in the name of "innocence"
will not build the fence you want,
it's not a defense
against danger or stranger,
the friend or foe
whose hands want to know
the feel of your child
your baby girl or maybe
your boy, a toy for their
yearning for violence, depravity
the gravity
of which will pull your child
into wild denial
her pain untamed
by your drugs prescribed,
or her drugs street-dirty. . . .

nothing can offer relief
from the reality that you

failed and jailed
her happiness in a grave
too deep for forgiveness

the false innocence
you render for them
by censoring truth
protects only you

the word

The opposite of innocence
is not sin,
despite what you're told
the Bible says.

Don't get me started
on the real meaning of
"abomination,"
or the contradictions,
omissions the bishops let slide
or translation errors,
or the scribes who lied.

(Eve ate the apple
because Adam
was afraid,
for the record.)

The opposite of innocence
is not sin. Dearly beloved,
the opposite of innocence
is strength.

wired together

Movie shoots bedazzle authors
even one set at a grimy high
school in Columbus, Ohio,
96 degrees
9,000 percent humidity
air-conditioning shut down
for reasons unknown.

I tried to stay out of the way,
slowly melted into a puddle
of author sweat, worrying about making
mistakes, even though the story
was all mine.

The electrician hunted me down.

He looked like the guy in the Dire
Straits video "Money for Nothing."
'Member him?
He looked like my great-uncle;
big square guy,
head like a paint can,

hands the size of catchers' mitts,
smelled like work

He found me standing
at the back of the infernal gym
next to a table covered
with cables and rolls of black, sticky tape.
He put down his tools and studied
his calloused hands,
cleared his throat, and whispered,
"I'm Melinda."

I wasn't sure I heard him right.
His iron-gray eyes
met mine. Ten thousand volts
arced through the air
then he spoke louder,
"I am Melinda,"
and I could hear
I could see the little boy hiding
inside him.

I stuttered,
twitching in the electric

atmosphere, wishing
I had the right words.

He wasn't there for a chat.
He picked up a roll
of black, sticky tape
meant for insulating,
for holding things together,
and said,
"A lot of us working on this film
are like her,
cuz, you know"—
he blinked and the tears escaped—
"it happened to us, too "

unraveling

"I know better," she said
"I *should* have known better"
this tapestry of a girl
the fabric of her world
unraveling

she said, "I threw up while he raped me
and he rolled me over
so he could keep going.
Who does that?" she asked
thread by thread stitching
the whos to her whys to the hows

she said, "He didn't just rape my body;
he broke the concrete
of all the sidewalks, so I trip
when I walk to class;
he poisons the air in the cafeteria
with the laughter of his friends.
I am falling apart at the seams,
unstrung, undone, torn to shreds."

her new sorority has millions of sisters
stitching thread with needles
sharpened on wombstones
embroidery hoops carved from hip bones
patterns whispered girl
child to girl child
sewing sightless words
coding the path to survival
counting the bodies and souls
with stitches as fine as whispers

but cloth, ill-woven and untested
warp and woof never quite locking
prevent memory's tapestry
from ever being completed
so
she will change that by mending
the tears, repairing the patchwork
of her life with new patterns,
stronger knots
she'll pull herself together
become the quilt assembled by loving hands
threaded with intention,
she'll start weaving her truth
by unbuttoning her mouth

#MeToo

Me, too weak to fight him off
me, too scared, silent
me too, disassembled by the guy
who . . . .

mis understood
mis taken
men tion my name
to my mi sery siblings
as we support
report
reveal the violence
they desperately want
us
to conceal.

Me to be stronger,
you to stand taller,
we to shout louder
than they thought
we could

keys

It wasn't a bad idea to go to his house
you've known him forever, he passed
out in your kitchen one night
middle of the party
(you gave him a pillow and puke bucket
and he washed both the next day)
you met his parents at homecoming
they liked you
he ordered pizza and is dying to game
on his new console, he made margaritas
cuz they are your fave
you can trust him.

He didn't say his roommates
were gone for the weekend
but hey,
you know the rules, you've stood
under the social media waterfall of pics
and videos of women defending themselves
how to fight back when attacked
in the dark, car keys between fingers
Wolverine claws ready in an alley,

when the stranger approaches
you're the superhero
sound effects floating above your head,
kick him in the balls
you are empowered
to smash his throat, shove his nose bones
into his brain, so easy.

And Squad rules, right?
We girls watch out for each other
monitor our drinks, emergency signal
flares if we need rescuing, no one leaves the club
with a stranger unless GPS tracking
is turned on and check-in times assigned
we are strong
we take care of each other.

But this isn't that cuz
he's not that guy,
he's a buddy, and a friend of a bunch of friends
he's a friend squared, cubed, and he hands you
the margarita laced
with GHB or ketamine or Rohypnol
as he takes the controls, turns on
his game

and you wake up
the next day broken
bruised confused contused confounded
astounded by the pain inside and out
cuz the rules they fed you
were the wrong tools
car keys clutched in tiny fists
never work.

Yourdick™

Yourdick™ is not as special as you want it to be
it's not a cannon, or a gun, or that football
spiral-thrown, fired
over all the players on the field, launched
from the dreams of your parents
into the arms of the boy
fast enough to break away from the pack,
nimble enough to tiptoe between sideline and
end zone,
the boy
man enough to get hit
and **hit** and **hit** and **hit**
and **hit** and **hit** and **hit** and **hit** and **hit and hit
and hit**
as they pile on until the whistle blows.

I know this is confusing,
you grew up on beer commercials that taught you
the equation of beer plus football equals sex,
and when beer is chugged
not to mention Jack, Stoli, or Fireball
spiced with the pills in your buddy's pocket

you feel entitled to score, to dominate
the other team—

Don't. Sex is not a game
where one person wins by destroying the other.
The overpowering of resistance
belongs only on the field
where the center of attention is a football
not Yourdamndick™.

forgiveness

Take your age the first time a stranger touched
your body with danger in his hands,
evil-minded. . . .

But it's not usually a stranger, is it?

Most times you think you know him,
but not really,
   if it was your brother, your uncle, grandfather,
   your
   dad
   who turned monster
   when he was alone with you;
   your
   teacher, priest, boss, date, best friend, best friend's
brother, best friend's father, coworker, president,
housemate, professor, butcher, CEO, talent scout, lab
partner, dentist, photographer, bus driver, clown,
band director, coach, pastor, scout leader, congress-
man, youth pastor, lawyer, mentor, regional manager,
neighbor, conductor, committee chair, rabbi, hero,
therapist, ski instructor, pediatrician,

the dad of the kids you babysat, who volunteered
to drive you home
the boy you were falling in love with
the dude in your fantasy soccer league
who turned into a monster
when he was alone
with your body.

Are you still doing the math?
Raise your number to the power
of three
exponentially increasing the impact
of his shackling hands
cuz you still feel them

The exits were blocked,
so you wisely fled your skin
when you smelled his intent,
like a selkie, you shed your pelt
and hid in the smoke without breathing

Multiply your number by the number of years
(or months or days, maybe hours)
before you spoke up about
the molestation fondling forcible touching

being chased to the door, promised the part
offered a higher grade, had your career
threatened,
your kids threatened,
man-handled against the wall
onthecouchthefloorthegroundthedesk
dirty words spit in your hair
the twisting of your arm
cuz he can't come until you cry

Now multiply that number by the number of times
you endured being harassed,
   hit on, talked down to, catcalled, gossiped about,
called a prude, slut-shamed, roofied, spied on
through the window, grabbed on a train, or had
another loser show you his dick in the park
   or on the bus
   or in a pic sent to your phone, unasked for

study that number,
and no matter what it is,
forgive yourself
because no, my friend,
you are not overreacting.
Not one bit.

banish

she wrote in tiny letters
that she was not
outkasted
for the exact same reason
that melinda
got outkasted
but
outkasting is hurtful
no matter
who you are
or what happened

triptych

a girl at a private school
on the West Coast
was raped at a party
raped by two boys
she once thought were friends

she limped home, called the police
who charged the rapists
who got out on bail
and kept going to school
her school
she rode the bus home, called the lawyers
who got a restraining order requiring
the rapists to stay two hundred feet away
which screwed up their schedules
and irritated the administrators
who made her eat lunch
in the library after that

One of my favorite images in *Speak* is Melinda
at her mother's store, where she folds
the wings of the triple-paneled mirror

around her
The Now in front of her
The Past to her left
and to her right
The Possible

Sorrow caught that girl halfway
through her junior year, bit her heels
hard, ripped out her Achilles tendons
hobbling her, those boys got probation
for raping her at the party
she got high for years, damaging
herself beyond recognition

for Melinda, the reflections multiply
endlessly distorting the way she sees
herself
kaleidoscoping her beating heart
warm breath fogging the glass

it took years, but that girl finally stopped
getting high, got her degree and a factory job
she tried college, but the PTSD dragged her home
which felt safer
the two boys who raped her graduated on time

went to college, got married
moved away, and started over
pretending they were clean slates.

Melinda's trick is looking hard
in the mirror, absolving herself
and cracking open doors to the next place,
but the girl at that school, so haunted,
smashed all the reflections, boarded
up the windows, and bolted the doors
forever stuck at fifteen years old
judged to serve a life sentence
for what they did

overheard on a train

"You just let him
do it
cuz if you don't
his friends talk
shit about you
online"

she wiped
at the rainfall
of tears, but they
drowned her
before the train could stop

Danuta Danielsson

We're all born to fight
but few are ever trained,
instead they tell us
"Be nice."

Danuta's mother survived
a Nazi concentration camp
alive but scarred,
so when the Nazis marched
through her Swedish town in 1985,
Danuta hauled back
and smacked a Nazi
in the head with her purse.

It was a big purse.

She snapped, they said
couldn't take it anymore
reached her breaking point.

We should teach our girls
that snapping is OK,
instead of waiting
for someone else to break them.

musing

Ophelia and Persephone walk into a coffee shop
bringing with them the smell of cinnamon
and rain.
"Latte?" asks Ophelia.
Persephone nods. "With an extra shot. You?"
"Earl Grey, hot, with room."

I turn off my music, keep the earbuds in, type
gibberish so I can spy
they shoot rock-paper-scissors
for who pays the bill.
Persephone wins, grins, orders scones with jam.
Ophelia leaves a huge tip.

Unwilling avatar for silenced girls, our Ophelia,
seen only though the male gaze;
pale gray construct constantly
throwing herself at boys and rivers. Found
a few strands of her hair on a berry bush
which I plucked and wove into the tapestry
unconscious, she later sprang from my forehead,
fully formed, as Melinda.

They chatter softly, unaware or uncaring
of the hungry looks
thrown their way from the men and the boys
envying the steam curling
around the girls' faces. They butter and jam
the scones, erupt into laughter over a private joke.
They speak
their own language, those two.

I ran into Persephone's mom years ago
at the grocery store, both of us worried
about our daughters,
all the daughters, captured by the underworld
and pulled out of sight. Demeter wiped my tears
and fed me pomegranate seeds
which I swallowed whole. Their taste flooded
back in my mouth when Lia awoke, the wintergirl
~~grateful to talk~~ mad at me for listening.

My coffee stone-cold, fingers cramped
from typing
it's time to head home,
walk back through the woods.
As I gather my tools, the girls quiet fall
into each other's eyes,

fingers entwined on the crumbs
knuckles satined with jam and butter
Persephone tucks a lock of Ophelia's hair
behind the shell of her ear and
Ophelia takes Persephone's hand and gently
kisses the palm.

I grin and close the door behind me.

anatomy

But anyways
I've got a bone to pick with you
Ken doll
about your bone, or rather the lack
of your bone, boner, or any boning tools,
not to mention a piss stick,
cuz I grew up with a small black-and-white
television before cable,
only three channels
(and PBS, which made my Republican mother
suspicious)
plus the wrench we used to turn the dial,
which broke two houses earlier—
we had limited options for knowledge.

But anyways, cuz I was raised in a plastic-wrapped,
white-bread-and-mayonnaise,
sexless world,
one sister, no brothers, two puritan parents,
all of my anatomical knowledge of boys
came from you, Ken,

you dickless wonder.
I was so confused!
I had friends who had brothers
so I knew boys had a . . .
THING
and that the THING was their kryptonite
cuz if a boy got fresh
(this confused me, too, cuz "fresh" was a word
that belonged next to "lettuce" or "eggs")
I was supposed to kick them between the legs
because the THING
was apparently quite fragile
and kicking it would really hurt
and the boy would leave me alone. One time
this came up at the dinner table
(at the parsonage: nice tablecloth, candles—just
picture it)
and my father, coughing loudly, red-faced,
said I should always punch him in the gut first
and reserve
THING-kicking to the very last,
if the boy was so stupid
that my punch didn't scare him off.

But anyways, I took off your clothes,
Ken.
A lot.
I studied between your legs, front and back
baffled
cuz I was pretty sure
that the vaguely putty-colored,
plastic, flat surface of your crotch
was not the THING
of playground lore
or my father's discomfort.

My imagination tended toward castles
and dragons and talking mountains,
not your junk.
Not even after my own Barbie bits—
boobs, butt, bulbous bodacious
babeness
(check yourself, Ken; I was eleven
when that shit went down)—
not even after I "blossomed"
to quote my father's excruciating phrase,
did I understand the THINGness.

You see, I remained for years
pig-ignorant of its precise geography.

So you can imagine my surprise
when I finally got comfortably naked
with a sexual partner fully equipped with a
THING and I turned on the light to study
this specimen.
(It must be noted that the THING wilted a bit
under the spotlight's glare, but later rallied.)
And I was shocked, shocked I tell you,
to discover that the THING, while definitely rooted
in the body's southern hemisphere
is not literally between your legs, but rather
proudly planted in the Brillo pad of pubic hair
that grows on the front lawn of your crotch.
Who knew?

But anyways, you let me down, Ken,
but I've made my peace with it. With you.
With the confused girl-child
who used to be me.

And Barbie? I've got nothing
to say to that bitch.
Not till she learns to walk
flat-footed,
like a real woman.

free the bleed

We bleed with the moon
near half our lives
but still
some guys think it's freaky
disgusting, unnatural

The location of the vagina
between where we pee
and where we poop
is a design flaw, maybe,
but it doesn't account for the shaming
for the sense that somehow women
are weaker
or foul
or damned
because we bleed once a moon

our bodies are muddy rivers
overflowing the banks to fertilize the fields,
hurricaning oceans with the energy
of time, tide, and galaxies,

silver ice caps defying the sun's
feeble attempts to melt us
we bleed and grow stronger

some of us breed, pouring blood
into love, planting his seed in our egg
creating life and feeding it
our red-coated strength
birthing in a torrent of salt
and blood
we are mountains

don't call it a period:
call it an
exclamation point

shame turned inside out

Sisters of the torn shirts.

Sisters of the chase
around the desk,
casting couch, hotel
room, file cabinet.
Sisters dragging
shattered dreams
bruised hopes
ambitions abandoned
in the dirt.

Sisters fishing
one by one
in the lake of shame;
hooks baited with fear
always come back empty.

Truth dawns slow
when you've been beaten
and lied to,

but it burns hard and bright
once it wakes.

Sisters, drop
everything. Walk
away from the lake, leaning
on each other's shoulders
when you need
the support. Feel the contractions
of another truth ready
to be born: shame
turned
inside out
is rage.

callout

we're sisters of the march
you and me
heavy backpacks digging
through our skin, bloody footprints
evidence of the miles we've walked

it happened to you, too
I know it did

that's why I'm so confused
I see your scars, that flinch around your eyes
when another dude loud-plows over your words
cuts you off from the herd on purpose
stands too close, drags your name to his fame
eats our time by not sharing the mic
gets paid twice as much for half the work
flirts with girls trust-blinded and excited
cuz he's buying the drinks

it happened to you, too
I know it did

but when the evidence of another victim
is presented
bruised, battered, dented, and shattered
you snort derision, bark suspicion
envisioning our past world
where girls had to shut up and take it
like you did, unsupported in even ordinary ways
never daring to report or demand a criminal
court investigation, no—you sneer
even though her flirtation was not an invitation
to degradation
he raped her
and you, still bleeding decades later
aren't healed enough to help, instead
you've become that bitch pissing on our sisters
in a feeble, feline climb to the top
claws out

it happened to you, too
I know it did, I can smell it
I see how pain frames your crooked smile,
that quick shift to defense,
chin up, fists ready

I'm sorry you didn't get the help you needed
you deserved a soft afghan wrapped around you
people to hold your hands
while you learned to walk again
so stand with us now
let's be enraged aunties together
enthroned crones, scythes blazing
instead of defending these men
who laugh at you when you turn your back
lean on me

ignore stupid advice

Don't get killed
Don't get robbed
Don't get billed for jobs
that were abandoned.

Don't let your house burn
or your pipes burst
or your children curse
Don't let your purse get stolen.

Don't get trapped underwater
Don't get food poisoning or the flu
(for God's sake, get vaccinated)
Don't get cancer, seriously,
do not get cancer.

Don't get T-boned by a drunk
Don't get struck by lightning
Don't get allergies
Don't get depressed
Don't get noticed by the IRS

Don't get catfished
or gaslit
Don't get ghosted by an ex
Don't get talked into a bigger car
Don't get bitten by a rabid dog
Don't get your boo angry
Don't get cheated on

Don't get called out
dragged
tagged in pics
you don't remember

Don't get raped
cuz the jackasses and idiots will say
that's your fault, too.

The Reckoning

The Reckoning
is born as whispers
which turn into snowflakes
melt into rainn
weep onto quiet fields
wake seeds
buried in the shit.

Dad-men, madmen,
fathers of daughters unpowered
by your brothers of the hunt
your bull and guilt,
creeping filth
like a five-o'clock shadow
you're afraid.

The Reckoning feeds
seeds that stretch in the night
to eat the dark
drink the moon
demand the dawn

claim the sun
rub it on our skin
soak it into our bones.

So afraid, manly men, you're unmade
by the mirror,
horrified cuz no matter how hard
you try, how loud the cheers amplified
by a surround-sound system
of institutional lies
you can still hear us.

The Reckoning
transforms us into tigers
hunting you down
one by one,
dragging you by the nape
of your dirty necks
to face her
face him
face them
the souls possessed of the bodies you stole
for what you thought was just a few minutes.

And after the crop is harvested
the fields cleared of rocks and stubble
swords beaten into plowshares
dirt furrowed
the new seeds, planted deep and cared for,
will grow into strong children
with kind hands and strong bodies
and honorable hearts
the first generation unscarred
untouchable
that's your loss
and our triumph

sincerely,

Maybe we're going about this the wrong way.

Maybe we should shout
out to all the dudes who didn't rape
us. Or even try.
Let's celebrate those
who ask permission
before touching and
—*get this*—
respect the answer!

High five, you lovable hunk of manhood!
You true Warrior of the Sword!
Thanks for not slipping me a roofie!
So grateful you didn't gang-rape
me with your roommates!
I didn't get herpes
from you, because you are so awesome
you didn't hit
me, then shove your dick in my mouth!
You rock!

A brave new world
of greeting cards
dawns.

Dear Boss,
       Just a heads-up to let you know
       I'm sending flowers
       to your mother
       to tell her how wonderful you are
       because you've never pulled out your dick
       and masturbated in front of me.

Dear College President,
       I am proud to announce that none of my
       professors
       this semester
       tried to force me to blow them.
       Those lawsuits have made a difference!
       Great job! Keep it up!
       (Sorry about that pun.)
       (Actually, no. Not sorry at all.)

It's not just what you say, but how
right?

not responsible for contents

The letter came from a prison
on the first page the man wrote
that he read *Speak,*
then he spoke, wrote his trauma, his boy
body the toy of an uncle for so long
that his Before It Happened was too short
to remember

on page two he wrote more
furtively, turning his hurt
into hunger, thundering, covering
the truth of his circumstances
the accusations of his molestation
of his stepdaughters, all
of them under seven years old
he told a tale of justice failed,
jailed innocent, he declared
wondering why the world
had turned against him
line after scrawled line
he mounded his hurts into a bonfire
of his vanities to burn

out the damning and hide
his crimes in smoke

I dug around, found the other side
to the story, before his trial
he confessed on Facebook
that a *different person*
lived inside of him
and that the *different person*
might . . . have hurt . . . the girls,
maybe,
if it happened, he was sorry
sort of

the jury convicted him in sixty minutes
the judge sentenced him to ninety years
in prison
where he scribbles with a poison pen

when you get a letter from jail
the envelope is stamped
"Not Responsible for Contents"
but somehow,
we are

Catalyst

I wrote a book about a girl who loves chemistry
a cross-country runner, preacher's daughter
only applies to MIT, and well, complications ensue
she's a little like me, but not much
to the outside world, it seems her life is perfect
but she's got a hole in her heart, panic in her veins
dread stalking close
she runs to stay ahead of it

her name is a wayfinder
Kate—the sound of an ax splitting wood
Malone—which is "one," "lone"
"alone" and "Ma," if you look close enough,
her mother died a long time ago
and that ache will never go away

I knew that Kate's *I'm fine!* mask was suffocating
but I didn't know what would convince her
to take it off
she needed a catalyst
that spark, a goad to force her out of her shell
so she could see herself for the very first time

one night, after hours of scribbling
and throwing out pages,
frustrated with my Kate quandary, I doze-dreamed
fingers dribbling sand by the ocean
of my imagination
I watched
as a new girl appeared

an angry girl
hands fisted out of habit
toes scuffing the dirt
in the yard;
dirt on the floor
grease on the stove
grime on her body
left by her father
the smelly girl
who everybody looks at
but nobody ever sees

Teri Litch

her last name means "corpse"
readers bewitched by a book
rarely peek under the lid of names

to the stewpots of boiling imagery below
but I need to taste a name's marrow
to write a character to life

kids like Teri Litch
don't have running water at home
they go unnoticed until the smell is unavoidable
and a kind teacher
offers to help with the laundry
and the faculty quietly collects canned food
so lunch won't be her only meal

few realized that the book
is really Teri's story, deliberately told
through Kate's cloudy vision
cuz Kate is still learning how to see
the girls are catalysts for each other
their collisions changing the course
of their lives,   friendship grows
in the most unexpected places

face my truth

This is not
a resting bitch face

This is
a touch-me-and-die face

a boy, a priest unholy

I was once a happy kid,
the man said
altar boy,
Boy Scout, shortstop
born on Sunday,
son and oldest brother

ten years old,
then eleven,
I loved the Lord our Father
Father Michael gave
me cup wine sip
wafer mouth open

he blessed me,
invited me
(special! so special!)
to the wreck room,
the re-creation room
wood-paneled basement lair
below the rectory

i was chosen
by the Lord,
father michael purred.
i had potential,
father michael told my parents
who never once asked
"Potential for what?"

the wreck room stank
of moldy clothes,
sweat and desperation
sweet wine and manipulation
vomit, candy, and exploitation
the taint of horror

he was a man of God
Christ, i thought
he was God

one night, my dad smelled
the stains on my uniform
from St. Michael the Archangel Elementary,
where father michael taught math
and subjects unholy in the wreck room

Dad's face a volcano
on the verge of eruption,
i explained
he stayed silent,
clock ticking on the wall
silent as he burned
my uniform in the trash
barrel behind the garage.

He lied to Mom, said he wrecked my
uniform with bleach. My fault, he told her,
not his.
Not your fault, he told me
but don't say a word
not a single word
to anyone.

Ever.

i still had to go to church
after that, though i stopped serving
at the altar, thank God.
When the time came
to kneel at the feet
of the priests

for Communion,
baby-boy bird mouth open
waiting to be sanctified

my dad knelt by my side.
My dad stared
at father michael feeding
me the Body and the Blood
with stained hands
my dad's heart thundered
like a volcano, hungry
to destroy.

I don't go to church anymore,
the man said. Not many do.
Infected by the angel-cloaked demons
whose hymns condemned us to darkness
with a smile;
we are legion.

loud fences

when I went to elementary school,
Wednesday afternoons
were for art projects and library books
and playing outside
because I wasn't Catholic
all the Catholic kids left after lunch on Wednesday
and walked to the parochial school down the block
for lessons from the priests and the nuns

everyone knew about the dangerous priest there
even kids like me who never met him
don't get caught in a room alone with that one,
they said
he liked hurting kids
bad and gross hurting
which is a good way to describe sexual abuse
when you're ten years old

I traveled to Australia a while back
to speak at conferences, schools, and libraries

and be astounded by everything
from kookaburras to Vegemite
my last stop on the tour was in Ballarat,
on the Yarrowee River

the school cancelcd my appcarancc
at the last minute
instead, I spoke at the public library
to a small group of kids
the librarian pulled me aside before handing
me the mic
she whispered that a sexual abuse scandal
was unfolding in town
and asked me to be sensitive about it

Ballarat had pricsts who likcd to bad and gross
hurt children
just like Syracuse. Just like Boston. Minneapolis.
Dallas.
Arizona, Iowa, Oregon, Wisconsin, California,
Kentucky, Colorado
Chile, Ireland, Austria, Canada, Guam
just like everywhere

in Australia alone, there are thousands of victims
countless suicides and immeasurable grief
the official investigation that began
the week I was in Ballarat
has now reached all the way to the Vatican

In Ballarat, like in so many other places
it wasn't one priest, it was many
generations of priests abusing
generations of children
In Ballarat, like in so many other places
some kids told their parents,
who confronted bishops
who moved the pedophiles
to new churches, new schools
where they had new flocks to prey on

But in Ballarat, unlike so many other places
something different happened

in Ballarat people tied colorful ribbons
to the fences
around the cathedral and the schools
where children
had been molested and raped

the ribbons loudly supported the survivors
of the predatory priests
and their families and everyone who loved them
the ribbons shouted that they were not alone
the ribbons announced that they were seen
the ribbons demonstrated that they were heard
the ribbons signaled revolution

more people tied ribbons to the fences
until all you could see were the colors,
not the iron rusting underneath
the church cut them off, but by morning
the fences were again beribboned
the church cut them off
the people put them back
then the ribbons spread to other cities,
other churches, other schools
across Australia and to other countries
all the way to the Vatican

in Ballarat those stubborn flags of hope
created Loud Fence; the term refers
to persistently, relentlessly reminding victims
of sexual violence
that they are important and supported and good

when I was in elementary school
and my friends walked
down to the church for their Wednesday lessons
I had to memorize poetry for a teacher
I chose "Mending Wall" by Robert Frost
about neighbors and the work of repairing
stone walls, of walling in and walling out
the famous line still opens itself in my head,
from time to time reminding that
"good fences make good neighbors"

in Ballarat,
good neighbors make loud fences
the language of love made visible

feralmoans

your brain, young thing
shadow-dancing with lightning
swimming, brimming with yearn, churn
and the sex! woo-boy! and hungers
you can't name yet, and crayon smells,
spells compelling, carouseling
under-skin earthquakes
altering your landscapes
eyesight, earhear changing every minute, dear
too close, too far, unplowed crowd
drowning, downing, drawn to
warm bodies like
a moth
to a flame

be careful
out there,
k?

emerging

wet-winged butterflies
wobbly antennae, shaky knees
their faces still lined
with chrysalis wrinkles
finally at liberty
straining to take flight

while terrified kings
reigning suspicious
witness the butterflies'
metamorphosis
effecting change
from elementary stasis
to fluttering chaos, launching
in the dawn's early fight
their unrestrained campaign
to remove politicians
from their paper palaces
bought and paid for,
the sad, recoiling kings
freak

because the otherworldly magic
available to the newly hatched
is boundless and unbreakable
which is why the powerful
won't let the young vote

But the kids know how to use matches

two opposites of rape

To have sex
is human.

To make love,
Divine.

yes, please

"yes"
sounds like heaven falling from the sky
yes smells like hot, hot
sweet apple pie
yes dances hip to hip, eye to eye
sober, yes
demands very sober, cuz yes shares this body
touch me
with permission only, yes—signed, sealed
deliverance from evil, no sin to be
tempted, but only with yes in the sheets
yes in the backseat, yes to a condom
yes, please go down on me until yes!
because yes is not swipe right, yes is hello
I want to get to know
you because maybe we
might yes, but the dance comes first, yes
the interplay of hey, flirt, hey, the pounding heart
of questioning yeses and nos, let's go
slow
revolyestionary notion

that behold, this body and soul
that yes welcomes yes embraces yes
the taste of someone who has proven
worthy
of your yes
is worth the questing, slow beckoning
interrogating, interesting, conversating
adventuring yes is ongoing
yes enthusiastic
yes informed
yes free-given
yes the truest test
of sex
the consent of yes is necessary

Ultima Thule

I speak at book festivals
to thousands of teens
and hundreds of brilliant teachers
who clutch 32-ounce cups of coffee
with extra shots of espresso and patience

I tell my stories, burning hot and angry
gentle some truths so the kids can hear them
drop consent bombs they can't avoid
laugh about the dumb things I've done
so they can laugh, too

Over three days, I sign countless books
and listen as girls speak
up about being raped
or molested or shared
or any of the varieties
of sexual violence visited
upon the young and wordless

Greenland is a dependency of Denmark,
if you travel to the far north of Greenland

then a little farther still
you might find the mythic land of Ultima Thule
home to the wind, ice, and lichen old as time
Ultima Thule, my refuge
for when the world gets too real
like when a twelve-year-old tells me
about Mommy's boyfriend
and the things he made her do
at night
when Mommy worked the late shift
after she wipes her tears on my shoulder
and promises to write
and walks back to her teacher

I whisper
Ultima Thule

empty and cold and holding a place for me
for cryotherapy, for vacuum-sealing myself
in the ice, just for a little while
imagining all the layers of clothes
I'd wear on Ultima Thule
the benign joy of studying polar bear songs
or renegade glaciers

dreaming of the aurora borealis
at the top of the world
and how I could make room
on Ultima Thule for anyone else
who just needs a space safe enough
to breathe, for a little while
like this girl
whose mommy broke up with that boyfriend
but now they have to live in their car

adaptable heart

the names of the charred survivors
who don't know how fucking tough
they are
nestle
hidden
in the fifth chamber
of my heart.

Their courage warms
me from the inside,
stubborn candles
illuminating
this scorched
pumpkin.

three

my peculiar condition arboreal

After they stole the mountains from the Mohawks
and thrashed the British, my grandfather's
people tapped sugar maple trees,
generations of us bled maple sap, wearing tamarack
snowshoes, under a late winter moon
spring urges rising, boiling
gallons of sap in iron vats
sold it cheap to neighbors, jacked
the price for outsiders who vacationed
in the woods where my grandfather roamed,
ax and rifle at the ready.

A quiet forest ranger
he taught me how to listen to the pine,
broad oak, woeful elm, sistering beeches,
spruce and fir for Christmas trees
and ironwood for fences
miles of paper birch tattooing memory
on their skin with black walnut ink
he gently pressed my palms
against the bark
so I could feel their whispers.

Ganoderma applanatum

Ganoderma applanatum is a fancy
way of saying the fungus you find
on some trees in the North, a boil,
canker sore, wide as a working man's hand,
a worry bursting from the hip
of an uprighteous beech

skyside watertight, wind-thick, wood-tough
bird-stained, blight-wrinkled
folding over and over on herself
like a slow-growing mountain
or a hand-forged sword

earthside, underside, dirtside
clean as a patient page
waiting
for a dreamer
to make her mark

sweet gum tree, felled

Ernest Boy Scout troop
awkwardly erecting small flags,
blue and gold, on deadfall
branches propped upright
with rocks, while a white-haired woman
cooks the boys' dinner over an open fire,
white-haired man sharpening a chainsaw
with a rat-tail file, properly,
with long, smooth strokes,
echoes of his wife, slowly stirring the pot.

The other men? Troop masters and dadfriends
slump-dressed for Saturday, clustered coffeeing,
watching one of their own revving
the other chainsaw, two-stroke oil smoking,
blade deadly dull and ready to kick, hungry
for legs, not wood, but this dad-dude
is clueless in sneakers, not boots,
blind to his need for protection, so damn tough
he leaves his headphones on the stump,
safety glasses, too. He squeezes the trigger

and the chain spins faster, motor screams,
oil smokes, and the other men lean
into the illusion of power
becoming more deaf
by the minute. But the saw, it sticks, bucks,
won't cut right, so the dad-dudes complain
and curse the machinery,
glancing at their phones.

The boys who pledge their allegiance
openhearted play
with sticks and stones
watching close.

The white-haired man, finally satisfied
puts down his tools, while the white-haired
woman
in steel-toed boots
puts on her safety glasses and headphones.
She starts the chainsaw with a single pull
looks at the old man, her husband or lover,
and he grins, knowing what comes next;
the old woman saws through expectations

and the sweet gum trunk like butter,
wood chips spitting at the openmouthed
dad-dudes unable
to process the sight.

piccolo

She hated being a six-foot-tall woman
in 1947, a freak of nature in a town
without a circus.
The class picture that year, organized by height
shows four tall boys, my Amazonian mother
then another twenty dudes, all smaller.
She wanted to play the piccolo
or at least the flute, delicate instruments
elegant, feminine testaments to belie her size
but the director gave her the trombone
cuz she
had the longest arms in the band.

She hunched, slouched with panache,
tried to shrink herself down
to the size of other girls, origami-folded
herself in upon herself, accidentally forging
a backbone that twisted
and misaligned her hips.

After days at school reducing her frame
and presence to blend into the bland expanse

of North Country expectations, my mother
would go home and cross paths
with her father, who wouldn't stand
for his girl to bow to the will of others
he forced her to stand tall
erect
against the wall of the living room for an hour
each night, shoulders back far enough to kiss
the wallpaper, her chin lifted, tears pearling,
the ache intended to remind her
never to bend to the whims
of the small-minded

She hated every minute,
but she taught me the same way,
and when my daughters shot up and towered
over us both
their long arms, strong hands snatching
basketballs and softballs, playing trumpet,
slamming gavels,
leaping over mountains and storming castle walls,
my mother rested in their shade
and finally relaxed
into the shape of her own satisfaction.

lost boys

My mother's last supper was homemade
mac and cheese.
Tethered to her oxygen machine
she ate at the kitchen table
with Daddy, me, and my beloved,
we drank champagne for their anniversary
and ours
then helped her back into bed
because Death
was gently knocking.

Getting pregnant was easy for my mom.
Staying pregnant was near impossible.
Her womb rejected boys, the doctors said,
claimed her body created a hostile environment
for the male fetus.

Five never-born sons
Five unseen brothers
Five failure marks in Mom's column
of the marriage scorecard
Six decades of my father's disappointment

On the other hand, the inside of my mother
was mahogany-red
cozy for girls like me. I snuggled in, feasted,
watched movies through her belly button,
tasted her fear
at the five-month mark, the gallows mile marker
for the boys. She'd light another cigarette
slip her hand across her belly, the skin tent
between us,
and whisper a prayer.

I've always loved my ghost brothers; they are
wolves
patrolling the edge of my sleep. They keep me safe
from the worst of my nightmares
crushing the fear in their jaws,
then going back on patrol for more. I wonder
how much they know about our family
about the complicated mothering
of she who carried us inside her.

When I was little I had no idea
what she'd been through. She used to say
"Affection is a sign of weakness"
which totally baffled me because she could be

both affectionate and strong. I'd give anything
to understand all of the layers
of tragedy that forced
her shell to become so hard.

After Mom's last supper, that homemade
mac and cheese,
relatives from beyond the grave came calling:
her parents, grandparents,
and Mom's favorite dogs.
She greeted them with delight, chatted happily
as she drifted to sleep.

Hallucinations, the hospice nurse said,
but she wasn't there
when the five never-borns arrived: tall and strong,
salt-and-pepper hair, ice-eyed like Daddy,
high cheekbones like Mom,
and I knew it was time to release our mother
so she could cross the river home
to where the rest of the family was waiting.

tangled

I have two bookcases
filled to spilling
with balls of yarn entwined
with dreams and schemes
for a life creative
enough to knit, stitch
all my prayers into sweaters
and socks and hats,
I have a faded plastic grocery bag
brimming with my most
favorite skeins,
audacious schemes.

Kin unpinned, my mother
was 100 percent wool, unprocessed
and itchy as hell, a hair shirt unraveled
then rerolled like razor wire
—carefully—
into a porcupine abristle
with resentment,
protecting her underbelly

resisting all attempts to untangle
her complications.

That's the story I am dying
to knit together,
if I could only find
the pattern.

blood moon

I had my last period the month
before my mother died

but years later I still dream
about bleeding,
the alarming crotch trickle
racing to the toilet
berating myself
cuz I didn't replace the emergency
tampon in my purse

In the dream
I pull down my pants
cursing the useless, translucent
toilet paper
but I stop
cuz it's not blood,
not anymore

The only thing that flows from my womb
in that dream

and in this waking
is thick, dark ink
word-fertile and raw

ordinary damages

My father lived for five years after my mother died
nobody was more surprised about this than he
three days a week, I'd pick him up at dawn
and we'd head to the gym, where I'd work out
while he sat on the bench, coffee in hand
charming the ladies
then we went to the diner for a delicious,
unhealthy breakfast, I'd read the paper,
he did the crossword puzzle in pen

and we talked
unrolling our family legacies
of trauma and silence
the stoicism that alternates with rage
the kindness that hides anxiety
the struggle to balance darkness with light
walking in the world and hiding from it
the cost of numbing pain,
the weariness of wrestling
the hungry need for forgiveness
the redemption of offering it with no strings

my nephew came home from Afghanistan
in the middle of those years
lots of soldiers from our village were returning
looking much, much older than when they left
I realized that their children would be crippled
by the ghosts of their parents' war
like I was. I wrote *The Impossible Knife of Memory*
with those kids in mind. I talked about the book
to my father all the time. He approved,
knowing full well
it was ripped from the pages of our lives.

My favorite scene in that book
takes place in the graveyard
where Hayley ponders the impact of the dead
on the living
how the things once done shape
the not yet dreamed of
she learns how to remember
without being destroyed

Before she died, my mother told me that Daddy
had been institutionalized
diagnosed as manic-depressive
when he was studying

to be a preacher and she worked to pay the bills.
This was right after he beat her
and broke her teeth,
when the ghosts and the dust of war cycloned
through him
and pushed him over the edge.
After that asylum stay
he never received counseling or medication
or therapy
instead, he gutted it out on his knees in prayer
and in long walks by the Erie Canal, begging
for the strength to stay alive

I am eternally, ridiculously grateful
that he found it.

At the end of his life, my father's mind frayed
at the edges
sometimes the ghosts appeared to be real,
as the veil between the worlds grew thin.
His heart was tired, too.
When a cardiologist suggested a pacemaker
Daddy asked if it would clear the fog
from his brain,
erase the hallucinations, and tame the monsters

busy throwing off their chains,
opening the army trunks
where the real horrors were buried
the doctor said possibly, but probably not

My father stood and said,
"I will not live without my mind,"
then shook the doctor's hand and told me
it was time to go home.

beeched

Beech forests dance
so slowly, only the wind
can see their grace
patterns slow-gliding
synchronized swans
on a still, dark lake
of dirt

Most trees take care of each other
and the beeches are no exception.
Underground tendrils secretly feed
the girl rooted in the sterile glacial till,
old ones lean to the side
so the boy burned by lightning
gets more sun than his brothers.

Survival of the fittest
is a recipe for loneliness,
the beeches susurrate
if you know how to listen,
guaranteeing a nasty life,

brutish and short. When one
suffers,
all are weakened,
but when everyone thrives,
we dance.

say my name

Halse rhymes with faults
assaults, vaults
halts close to scalds
and haunts
then salts confusion for the unwary
cuz no one can pronounce it
'cept kin

Names have roots deep
like family trees in graveyards
tapping endless wells
guarded by Norns, wyrd sisters
word sisters charged with our fates
Old English roots of
Halse
are tangled in *gehálsian*
a verb that means "to implore
or invoke the gods;
to speak,"
in Danish, *hals* means "throat"
William Chalker Halse
fled England in 1798

to Nova Scotia, where he married
a girl named Sarah
her last name
was
. . . . wait for it . . . .
Story
Sarah Story
if I put that in a novel, my editor
would make me cut
it out as too ridiculous to be true
but it is

Halse rhymes with waltz
watch me dance
and don't forget it

reminder

the wings of angels connect
to their backbones
just behind
their steadfast hearts

tree trunks connect
sun-breathing leaves
chlorphylling with life
to their roots, muddy-dark

the spines of books connect
page to page
writer to reader
teacher to student
page to page
past to future
pain to power
page to page
rage to peace

this note about anatomy
from me

to you
is for the remembering
that after you speak

after you shout
your open mouth
will breathe in
the light for which
you've hungered

and your backbone
will unfurl until
you can again dance
to the beat
of your steadfast
heart

POSTLUDE: my why

stories entertain
engage, outrage
uplift, help us
overcome
our troubles

writing rage-poems by the sea
pen, hands, claws stained with ink
until the bottle runs dry
and then I write in blood, spit, and fire
lantern's light in the mirror
scattering the dark

stories activate, motivate,
celebrate, cerebrate,
snare our fates
and share our great
incarnations of hope

thanks for listening.

Resources for Readers

SEXUAL VIOLENCE

RAINN: RAINN (Rape, Abuse & Incest National Network)
is the largest anti-sexual violence organization in the
United States of America. In partnership with more than
1,000 local sexual assault service providers, it operates the
National Sexual Assault Hotline: 800-656-HOPE (4673),
online.rainn.org. En español, rainn.org/es.

END RAPE ON CAMPUS: End Rape on Campus works to end
campus sexual violence by supporting survivors, education,
and policy reform. endrapeoncampus.org.

FORGE: FORGE is a national transgender anti-
violence organization. They help transgender, gender
nonconforming, and gender nonbinary survivors of sexual
assault. forge-forward.org.

IGNITE: IGNITE Supports survivors of sexual violence
and domestic violence who are Deaf, DeafBlind, or Hard of
Hearing. deafignite.org.

1IN6: 1IN6 supports male victims of unwanted sexual
experiences, sexual abuse, and sexual violence. 1in6.org.

NATIONAL SEXUAL VIOLENCE RESOURCE CENTER: A
national information and resource organization that works
with the Centers for Disease Control and Prevention to

collect and share resources with people and organizations
working to understand and eliminate sexual violence.
nsvrc.org.

MENTAL HEALTH

TO WRITE LOVE ON HER ARMS: To Write Love on Her
Arms works to help people who are struggling with
depression, addiction, self-injury, and suicide find help and
hope. twloha.com.

SUICIDE PREVENTION LIFELINE: National network
of crisis centers that offer free emotional support 24/7,
including specific resources for kids, LGBTQ+ people,
Native Americans, Deaf and Hard of Hearing people, loss
survivors, attempt survivors, disaster survivors, and veterans.
suicidepreventionlifeline.org. 800-273-TALK (8255)

THE TREVOR PROJECT: Crisis intervention and suicide
prevention for LGBTQ+ youth, offering a hotline (phone,
text, and online chat), and educational resources for family
and allies. thetrevorproject.org.

SAFE HORIZON: Offers resources to survivors of domestic
violence, human trafficking, child abuse, stalking, youth
homelessness, and domestic violence. safehorizon.org.

SUBSTANCE ABUSE AND MENTAL HEALTH SERVICES
ADMINISTRATION: This agency of the U.S. Department of
Health and Human Services provides services for people
struggling with mental health or substance abuse issues.
samhsa.gov.

Acknowledgments

The curious practice of turning ideas into poetry and poetry into a book like this one requires a chorus of people whose names must be shouted loudly.

All hail the patient copyeditors! Ryan Sullivan and Marinda Valenti tried their very best to keep me corralled with decent punctuation and grammar, but opened the gate to my stylistic quirks when I asked. The cover designer, Jessica Jenkins, and the designer of the interior, Nancy Brennan, created stunning art that amplifies my words—thank you!

Lindsay Boggs and Kaitlin Kneafsey are Publicity Miracle Workers. Thank you both for helping to put *SHOUT* into the hands of readers. I'd also like to give a huge shout-out (ha!) to Viking Books publisher Ken Wright, for his constant patience and kindness. A standing ovation goes to all of the other random Penguins who have been cheering on my work for nearly two decades, especially Jen Loja, Carmela Iaria, Erin Berger, Felicia Frazier, Emily Romero, Eileen Bishop Kreit, Shanta Newlin, Mary Raymond, and—last but not least—Trevor Ingerson. Being a part of your family makes me feel brave, and for that I am eternally grateful.

Tusind tak to Pernille Ripp, incredible teacher and founder of the Global Read Aloud (theglobalreadaloud .com) for kindly correcting my Danish spelling and grammar mistakes. Eric Gansworth (Onondaga), Lowery Writer-in-Residence at Canisius College, generously helped me work through the issue of properly centering the violence perpetrated on the Mohawk nation by settlers like my family. Thanks also to G. Donald Cribbs, counselor and author, who helped me develop the robust list of mental health resources.

My agent, Amy Berkower, has listened to me rant, fantasize, rage, and mutter for years, while waiting for books to be born. Thank you, dear friend, for your support and unflagging good cheer. Huzzahs to everyone else at Writers House, especially to Cecilia de la Campa, Executive Director, Global Licensing and Domestic Partnerships, for finding so many homes outside the United States for *SHOUT* and my other books. I'd also like to give an overdue shout of appreciation to Michael Mejias for his work to make publishing better reflect our country, and who warmly made me feel so welcome when I started working with Writers House.

The writing of this book began at the home of my buddies Greg Anderson and Sue Kressley. Thank you both for the space, the sunrises by the beach, and helping make our family whole. My assistant, Jenn Northington, is equal parts brilliant and magical; capable of creating time and space for me to do the working of writing—THANK YOU, Jenn! I could not have done this without you. My children and grandchildren are all poetry in motion. They are the light that keeps me going when darkness threatens. My sister-girl Deborah Heiligman is always there for me; in silence, in conversation, in disagreement, in growth, and in love. Thank you for everything, Debi.

This book would not, could not, have been written without the support and encouragement of my editor, Kendra Levin. She shall ever be called Kendra of the Keen Eye and Gentle Heart. Thank you, thank you, thank you, for helping me do this work, and for being such a warrior midwife.

Finally and forever, thank you to my oldest friend, my husband, Scot. Thanks for listening, for wiping away my tears, for bandaging my bruises, for supporting my art and my voice, and for lending me your strength when I couldn't find my own. *This world and the next, my love.*

SHOUT discussion questions

1. The introduction ends with the line, "This is the story of a girl who lost her voice and wrote herself a new one." What does it mean to write yourself a new voice?

2. Anderson opens the memoir with poems about her father and the trauma he carried from his time in the army during World War II. How is trauma passed from one generation to the next? How does it evolve? Why does the author explain what her father went through before describing the trauma she experienced as a young girl?

3. We see Anderson refusing to learn how to swim in "earthbound" (p. 17) before she dedicates herself to the sport in "practice" (p. 22). How does this journey relate to her life's work of speaking out against rape culture and supporting sexual assault survivors? What does it mean to "breathe without air" (p. 23)?

4. What power does "speaking up" or "speaking your truth" have in this memoir? What does it mean to *speak* versus *shout*?

5. *SHOUT* is told in free verse, which takes on a variety of poetic forms. What do you think the effect of the different structures in each poem is? What is the author able to say that she could not in traditional prose?

6. The collection of poems is largely arranged chronologically. Can you think of another way to arrange them? How would reading the poems in a different order change the experience or their meaning?

7. On p. 215, Anderson urges that "We should teach our girls / that snapping is OK, / instead of waiting / for someone else to break them." What do you think the author means by "snapping"?

8. Why do you think Anderson found her experience living abroad in Denmark to be so life changing? How did it differ from her life at home? How was it the same?

9. Choose an emotion that you think best describes this poetry collection, such as anger, hopefulness, sadness, or another word of your choosing. Explain your choice.

10. Conversations about sexual violence often ignore male victims. How might it be different for them to shout their truths?

11. In "POSTLUDE: my why" (p. 291), Anderson explores why she finds stories so powerful. What makes stories powerful in your opinion? What's your "why" that makes you want to shout?

Read more
by Laurie Halse Anderson!

A *NEW YORK TIMES* BESTSELLER AND
LONGLISTED FOR THE NATIONAL BOOK AWARD
The Impossible Knife of Memory

For the past five years, Hayley Kincaid and her father, Andy, have been on the road, never staying long in one place as he struggles to escape the demons that have tortured him since his return from Iraq. Now they are back in the town where he grew up so Hayley can attend school. Perhaps, for the first time, Hayley can have a normal life, put aside her own painful memories, even have a relationship with Finn, the hot guy who obviously likes her but is hiding secrets of his own.

Will being back home help Andy's PTSD, or will his terrible memories drag him to the edge of hell, and drugs push him over? *The Impossible Knife of Memory* is Laurie Halse Anderson at her finest: compelling, surprising, and impossible to put down.

"At turns heartbreaking, at turns funny, the narrative in this book is so spot on I wanted to give Hayley my phone number so she would have a friend in times of crisis. Seriously—does ANYONE write troubled teen characters with the realism, grace, and soul of Laurie Halse Anderson?"

—**Jodi Picoult,** *New York Times* **bestselling author of**
The Storyteller* and *Between the Lines

**THE *NEW YORK TIMES* BESTSELLING STORY OF
A FRIENDSHIP FROZEN BETWEEN LIFE AND DEATH**

Wintergirls

Lia and Cassie are best friends, wintergirls frozen in fragile bodies, competitors in a deadly contest to see who can be the thinnest. But then Cassie suffers the ultimate loss—her life—and Lia is left behind, haunted by her friend's memory and racked with guilt for not being able to help save her. In her most powerfully moving novel since *Speak*, award-winning author Laurie Halse Anderson explores Lia's struggle, her painful path to recovery, and her desperate attempts to hold on to the most important thing of all: hope.

"If you're a teenage girl, *Wintergirls* might just save your life."

—*Miami Herald*

**ANOTHER AWARD WINNER FROM
LAURIE HALSE ANDERSON!**

Catalyst

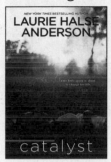

Meet Kate Malone—straight-A science and math geek, minister's daughter, ace long-distance runner, new girlfriend (to Mitchell "Early Decision Harvard" Pangborn III), unwilling family caretaker, and emotional avoidance champion. Kate manages her life by organizing it, as logically as the periodic table. She can handle it all—or so she thinks. Then things happen like a string of chemical reactions: first the Malones' neighbors get burned out of their own home and move in. Kate has to share her room with her nemesis, Teri Litch, and Teri's little brother. The days are ticking by and she's still waiting to hear from the only college where she's applied: MIT. Kate feels that her life is spinning out of control—and then, something occurs that truly blows it all apart.

Set in the same community as the remarkable *Speak*, *Catalyst* is a novel that will change the way you look at the world.

"Intelligently written . . . this complex, contemporary story carries much of the intensity and harshness of *Speak*."
                                                                        —*Kirkus Reviews*

A *NEW YORK TIMES* BESTSELLER

Twisted

High school senior Tyler Miller used to be the kind of guy who faded into the background—average student, average looks, average dysfunctional family. But since he got busted for doing graffiti on the school and spent the summer doing outdoor work to pay for it, he stands out like you wouldn't believe. His new physique attracts the attention of queen bee Bethany Milbury, who just so happens to be his father's boss's daughter, the sister of his biggest enemy—and Tyler's secret crush. And that sets off a string of events and changes that have Tyler questioning his place in the school, in his family, and in the world.

In *Twisted*, the acclaimed Laurie Halse Anderson tackles a very controversial subject: what it means to be a man today. Fans and new readers alike will be captured by Tyler's pitch-perfect, funny voice, the surprising narrative arc, and the thoughtful moral dilemmas that are at the heart of all of the author's award-winning, widely read work.

"Poignant and gripping."   **—*Kirkus Reviews***

Prom

Ashley Hannigan doesn't care about the prom, but she's the exception. It's pretty much the only good thing that happens in her urban Philadelphia high school, and everyone plans to make the most of it—especially Ash's best friend, Natalia, who's the head of the committee and has prom stars in her eyes.

Then the faculty advisor is busted for taking the prom money. Suddenly, Ash finds herself roped into putting together a gala dance out of absolutely nada. But she has help—from her large and loving (if exasperating!) family, from Nat's eccentric grandmother, from the principal, from her fellow classmates. And in making the prom happen, Ash learns some surprising things about making her life happen, too.

"Anderson finds humor and heartache in a situation that's pretty ordinary. But that's the key to the book's appeal: how normal it is, and real." **—*The Philadelphia Inquirer***